Beyond the shadows of fear

A Guide for fearleass living

By: Mustafa Nejem

CONTENTS

Chapter 1

The Anatomy of Fear:
Understanding Its Roots and Impact on Life

1. Identifying Fear Triggers:
Overview:
- Get it that fear can show in different shapes – from level-headed concerns to unreasonable tensions.
- Distinguish individual fear triggers – circumstances, considerations, or encounters that inspire fear.

Exploration:
- Reflect on past encounters where fear played a noteworthy part.
- Reflect on past encounters where fear played a noteworthy part.

Action Steps:
Mindful Observation:
- Create the hone of careful perception in challenging circumstances. This includes deliberately watching your enthusiastic reactions without quick judgment or response.
- Stop and take many profound breaths to center yourself, permitting you to impartially watch the feelings that emerge.

Emotional Check-Ins:
- Plan normal enthusiastic check-ins all through the day. Set alerts or updates to incite minutes of self-reflection.
- Inquire yourself questions like, "How am I feeling right presently?" or "What feelings are show in this minute?"

Journaling for Emotional Patterns:
- Utilize a devoted feelings diary to record your passionate responses in different circumstances.
- Note the setting, triggers, and the escalated of your passionate reactions. Over time, designs may rise, giving profitable experiences.

Feedback Loop:
- Look for criticism from others who may have watched your enthusiastic responses in particular circumstances.
- Useful criticism can offer an outside point of view, helping in a more comprehensive understanding of your enthusiastic reactions.

2. The Biological Basis of Fear:
Overview:
- Dive into the physiological angles of fear, counting the fight-or-flight reaction.
- Recognize that fear could be a characteristic and versatile reaction outlined for survival.

Exploration:
- Ponder the part of the amygdala and other brain locales in handling fear.
- Get it how adrenaline and cortisol impact the body amid fear.

Action Steps:
Hone mindfulness strategies to direct physiological reactions.
Lock in in standard physical action to oversee push hormones.

3. Cognitive Roots of Fear:
Overview:
- Look at how considerations and convictions contribute to the involvement of fear.
- Get it the affect of negative self-talk and silly considering.

Exploration:
- Distinguish restricting convictions that fuel fear.
- Investigate cognitive twists that increase on edge considerations.

Action Steps:
Challenge nonsensical convictions through cognitive rebuilding.
Develop positive certifications to check negative self-talk.

4. Emotional and Behavioral Manifestations:
Overview:
- Investigate how fear can show in feelings and behaviors.
- Recognize evasion and lingering as common fear-based behaviors.

Exploration:
- Analyze how fear impacts decision-making and interpersonal connections.
- Get it the association between fear and hairsplitting.

Action Steps:

Start with Awareness:
- A few time as of late successfully searching for trouble, create mindfulness of your reassurance zones. Recognize ranges where you tend to avoid challenges or where fear routinely rises.
- Recognize the feelings related with distress, and get it that it's a normal portion of development.

Gradual Exposure:
- Start with little and reasonable distress. This can be locks in in a discussion with somebody modern, attempting a unused movement, or confronting a minor fear.
- Slowly increment the level of inconvenience as you gotten to be more usual to pushing your boundaries.

Mindful Approach:
- Hone mindfulness methods, such as profound breathing or contemplation, when experiencing distress.
- Center on the show minute and watch your contemplations and sentiments without judgment.

Reflect and Learn:
- After grasping distress, take time to reflect on the encounter. What did you learn around yourself? How did you oversee the inconvenience?
- Utilize these reflections as openings for individual development and alter your approach in like manner.

5. The Impact on Life:
Overview:
- Look at how unchecked fear can restrain individual and proficient development.
- Get it the long-term results of living in a consistent state of fear.

Exploration:
- Reflect on missed openings and unfulfilled potential due to fear.
- Consider the affect of fear on connections, career, and in general life fulfillment.

Action Steps:

Define Clear Objectives:
- Clearly express your objectives, guaranteeing they are particular, quantifiable, achievable, pertinent, and time-bound.
- For example, if public speaking is a fear, a goal could be delivering a short presentation within the next month.

Identify Comfort Zones:
- Recognize and understand your existing comfort zones. These are areas where you feel at ease and may be resistant to change.
- Choose goals that intentionally challenge these comfort zones, fostering personal and professional growth.

Gradual Progression:
- Start with goals that are slightly outside your comfort zone and progressively increase the challenge level.
- The gradual approach allows for a smoother adjustment and helps prevent overwhelming feelings.

Align with Personal Values:
- Ensure that your goals align with your core values and long-term aspirations. This alignment enhances motivation and provides a meaningful context for the challenges you undertake.

Break Down Larger Goals:
- Break down larger, more daunting goals into smaller, more manageable steps.
- This incremental approach makes the process less intimidating and more achievable.

Regularly Review and Adjust:
- Periodically review your goals to assess progress and adjust them as needed. It's okay to modify goals based on changing circumstances or a deeper understanding of your fears.

6. Empowering Strategies for Fearless Living:
Overview:
- Explore various strategies to overcome and manage fear.
- Emphasize the importance of self-compassion and resilience.

Exploration:
- Investigate mindfulness practices, visualization, and positive psychology.
- Learn from individuals who have successfully navigated and conquered fear.

Action Steps:

Self-Reflection on Coping Strategies:
- Reflect on past experiences where you successfully coped with fear. Identify the strategies, techniques, or coping mechanisms that were effective for you.
- Recognize both internal (mindset, resilience) and external (tools, resources) elements that contributed to overcoming fear.

Research and Learn:
- Explore a variety of coping strategies and tools that are proven to help individuals manage fear.
- This could include mindfulness practices, deep breathing exercises, visualization techniques, or engaging in activities that bring a sense of calm.

Create a Comprehensive Toolkit:
- Compile a toolkit that incorporates a diverse range of strategies. Ensure it includes both short-term interventions for immediate relief and long-term practices for sustained growth.
- Your toolkit could also include inspirational quotes, affirmations, or personal notes to boost motivation.

Tailor to Personal Preferences:
- Recognize that everyone is unique, and what works for one person may not work for another.
- Tailor your toolkit to your personal preferences and inclinations.
- Experiment with different techniques and refine your toolkit based on what resonates with you the most.

Regularly Update and Expand:
- Treat your toolkit as a dynamic resource that evolves with your experiences. Regularly update it with new insights, strategies, or tools that you discover along your journey.
- Share your toolkit with your support network, inviting their input and suggestions.

Chapter 2

The Mind's Echoes:
How Fear Shapes Our Thoughts

1. Understanding the Cognitive Impact of Fear:
Overview:
- Recognize that fear has a profound impact on cognitive processes, influencing thoughts, perceptions, and decision-making.
- Explore the evolutionary purpose of fear in shaping cognitive responses for survival.

Exploration:
- Delve into cognitive psychology to understand how fear triggers cognitive biases and distorts perceptions.
- Investigate how the brain processes fear-inducing stimuli and the subsequent cognitive responses.

Action Steps:
Start with Basic Mindfulness Techniques:
- Begin your mindfulness journey with basic practices such as focused breathing or body scan meditations.
- Establish a regular mindfulness routine, dedicating specific moments each day to cultivate present-moment awareness.

Apply Mindfulness in Real-Time:
- During fear-inducing situations, consciously apply mindfulness techniques to observe your thoughts without immediate judgment.
- Focus on your breath, physical sensations, or the surrounding environment to anchor yourself in the present moment.

Body-Mind Connection:
- Pay attention to the connection between your thoughts and bodily sensations during moments of fear.
- Mindfully scan your body for tension, changes in heart rate, or other physical responses associated with fear.

Non-Judgmental Awareness:
- Cultivate a non-judgmental awareness of your thoughts. Observe them as passing phenomena without attaching labels of right or wrong.
- Allow yourself to experience the thoughts without getting entangled in them.

Progressive Exposure:
- Gradually expose yourself to fear-inducing situations, incorporating mindfulness techniques. Start with mildly challenging situations and progress to more intense scenarios.
- The goal is to build resilience and enhance your ability to observe thoughts without being overwhelmed.

2. The Intersection of Emotion and Thought:
Overview:
- Examine the interconnectedness of emotions, particularly fear, and thought processes.
- Understand how emotional responses can override rational thinking in the presence of fear.

Exploration:
- Explore case studies or real-life examples where fear significantly influenced decision-making.
- Consider the impact of chronic fear on long-term cognitive patterns and mental health.

Action Steps:
Self-Reflection on Emotional Responses:
- Regularly reflect on your emotional responses, especially during fear-inducing situations.
- Identify specific emotions and consider how they influence your thoughts, behaviors, and decision-making.

Emotional Vocabulary Building:
- Expand your emotional vocabulary to accurately label and articulate your feelings.
- The ability to pinpoint and express nuanced emotions enhances your understanding of the emotional landscape during fear-inducing moments.

Empathy Development:
- Cultivate empathy by seeking to understand the emotions of others. This practice enhances emotional intelligence and provides a broader perspective on how emotions shape thoughts.
- Engage in active listening and consider the emotions underlying the perspectives of those around you.

Mindful Observation of Emotions:
- Integrate mindfulness practices specifically focused on observing emotions. This involves non-judgmental awareness of emotional experiences as they arise.
- Mindful observation allows you to step back from immediate reactions and gain insights into the emotional undercurrents influencing your thoughts.

3. Fear-Based Thought Patterns:

Overview:
- Identify common thought patterns that arise in response to fear, such as catastrophizing, overgeneralization, or black-and-white thinking.
- Examine how these patterns contribute to a cycle of anxiety and self-perpetuating fear.

Exploration:
- Analyze personal experiences where fear has led to distorted thought patterns.
- Research psychological models that explain the cognitive mechanisms behind fear-based thinking.

Action Steps:

Choose a Dedicated Journal:
- Select a notebook or a digital platform specifically designated for your thought journal during fear-inducing situations.
- Having a dedicated space allows for focused reflection and easy tracking of patterns over time.

Record Triggering Situations:
- When faced with fear-inducing situations, immediately document the details in your journal.
- Include information about the context, people involved, and any other relevant factors contributing to the fear.

Describe Emotional Responses:
- Articulate your emotional responses in detail. Use descriptive language to capture the intensity and nature of your feelings.
- Note any physical sensations accompanying the emotions, such as tension, rapid heartbeat, or changes in breathing.

Document Thoughts and Automatic Beliefs:
- Write down your immediate thoughts and automatic beliefs during the fear-inducing moments.
- Be as specific as possible, capturing both the surface-level thoughts and any underlying assumptions or narratives.

Explore Past Experiences:
- Connect current thoughts and emotions to past experiences by exploring potential triggers rooted in earlier events.
- Reflect on whether there are recurring themes or patterns across different fear-inducing situations.

Note External Influences:
- Consider external influences that might contribute to your thoughts and emotions, such as societal expectations, cultural factors, or personal expectations.
- Recognize how external pressures may shape your perception of fear.

Track Changes Over Time:
- Regularly review entries to identify changes or patterns in your responses over time.
- Look for any shifts in the intensity of fear, alterations in thought patterns, or improvements in coping mechanisms.

4. The Role of Perception in Fear:

Overview:
- Investigate how fear alters perception, leading to heightened sensitivity and selective attention.
- Understand the role of confirmation bias in reinforcing fear-based perceptions.

Exploration:
- Explore studies on the impact of fear on visual and auditory perception.
- Consider how societal factors contribute to the shaping of collective fears and perceptions.

Action Steps:
- Engage in mindfulness exercises to observe how fear influences sensory perceptions.
- Actively seek out diverse perspectives to counteract the tunnel vision that fear can create.

5. Neuroplasticity and Rewiring Fearful Thought Patterns:
Overview:
- Explore the concept of neuroplasticity and its potential to rewire the brain's response to fear.
- Understand how intentional practices can reshape neural pathways associated with fear.

Exploration:
- Research studies on the brain's capacity to adapt and change through experiences and intentional interventions.
- Examine successful cases where individuals have overcome fear-induced thought patterns.

Action Steps:
- Engage in activities that promote neuroplasticity, such as learning new skills or adopting a growth mindset.
- Implement cognitive-behavioral strategies to actively rewire fear-induced neural pathways.

6. Mindfulness and Fear-Based Thought Observation:
Overview:
- Highlight the role of mindfulness in observing and detaching from fear-based thoughts.
- Explore mindfulness practices that specifically target the awareness of thoughts in the presence of fear.

Exploration:
- Investigate the impact of mindfulness on the brain's default mode network and its connection to fear modulation.
- Examine the use of mindfulness in therapeutic settings for individuals dealing with fear-related cognitive challenges.

Action Steps:
Structured Journaling:
- Create a structured thought journal specifically tailored for fear-inducing situations.
- Include sections for the date, the triggering event, associated emotions, thoughts, and subsequent behaviors.

Immediate Reflection:
- Journal as soon as possible after a fear-inducing situation occurs to capture immediate thoughts and emotions.
- This real-time reflection helps in identifying the raw and unfiltered responses to fear.

Identify Cognitive Patterns:
- Regularly review entries to identify recurring cognitive patterns or automatic thoughts associated with fear.
- Look for common themes, trigger points, and the intensity of emotional responses.

Use of Descriptive Language:
- Encourage the use of descriptive language in the journal. Detail the nuances of thoughts and emotions to enhance self-awareness.
- Consider incorporating adjectives that accurately express the intensity and nature of your feelings.

Track Behavioral Responses:
- Extend the journaling practice to include observations of your behavioral responses to fear.
- Note any avoidance behaviors, procrastination, or other actions taken as a result of fear-based thoughts.

Chapter 3

Fear's Physical Dimension: Recognizing Bodily Responses

1. Understanding the Physiology of Fear:
Overview:
- Delve into the physiological responses triggered by fear, known as the "fight or flight" response.
- Explore the role of the autonomic nervous system, specifically the sympathetic and parasympathetic branches.

Exploration:
- Investigate how fear activates the release of stress hormones such as adrenaline and cortisol.
- Understand the evolutionary purpose of the physiological response to fear for survival.

Action Steps:

Comprehensive Reading:
- Dive into reputable literature on the neuroscience, psychology, and biology of fear.
- Explore books, articles, and research papers written by experts in the field to gain a comprehensive understanding of the science behind fear-induced physical reactions.

Online Courses and Webinars:
- Enroll in online courses or attend webinars focused on the neuroscience of fear.
- Platforms like Coursera, edX, or universities often offer courses that provide in-depth insights into the physiological aspects of fear.

Documentary Exploration:
- Watch documentaries that explore the biological and psychological dimensions of fear.
- Documentaries can provide a visual and narrative perspective, enhancing your understanding of the complex interplay between the brain and the body during fearful experiences.

Podcast Listening:
- Explore podcasts featuring experts in psychology and neuroscience discussing fear and stress responses.
- Podcasts often offer accessible and engaging content, breaking down complex scientific concepts into more understandable terms.

Engage with Scientific Journals:
- Access scientific journals and publications that focus on fear research.
- Platforms like PubMed or specialized journals in psychology and neuroscience can provide access to the latest studies and findings.

2. Body-Mind Connection:
Overview:
- Explore the bidirectional relationship between the mind and body in the context of fear.
- Understand how thoughts and emotions influence physiological responses and vice versa.

Exploration:
- Investigate studies highlighting the impact of stress and fear on physical health.
- Explore mind-body practices that aim to harmonize the body-mind connection, such as biofeedback or psychophysiological therapies.

Action Steps:

Daily Mind-Body Journal:
- Establish a daily journal specifically dedicated to the connection between thoughts, emotions, and physical sensations.
- Record instances where specific thoughts or emotions coincide with distinct physical responses.

Emotion-Body Mapping:
- Create a visual or written map associating emotions with corresponding bodily sensations.
- Use color-coded or descriptive symbols to highlight the intensity and location of physical responses linked to specific emotions.

Pattern Recognition:
- Analyze journal entries over time to identify recurring patterns or correlations between certain thoughts, emotions, and physical sensations.
- Look for triggers that consistently lead to specific bodily reactions.

Mindful Body Scan Practice:
- Integrate regular mindful body scan sessions into your routine to deepen the awareness of physical sensations.
- Focus on systematically scanning each part of the body, noting any tension, warmth, or other sensations related to emotional states.

3. Recognizing Individualized Physical Responses:

- **Overview:**
  - Acknowledge that individuals may experience diverse physical responses to fear.
  - Explore how genetic factors, personal history, and cultural influences contribute to the variability in bodily reactions.

Exploration:
- Conduct a self-assessment to identify your unique physical responses to fear.
- Consider how cultural or familial perspectives on fear might shape your individualized reactions.

Action Steps:
- Keep a journal to document physical sensations during fear-inducing situations.
- Share experiences with friends or support groups to gain insights into diverse bodily responses.

4. Heightened Sensations and Sensory Perception:

Overview:
- Delve into how fear amplifies sensory perception and awareness.
- Explore studies on the enhanced sensory capabilities during states of fear.

Exploration:
- Investigate the role of the amygdala and other brain structures in heightening sensory perception during fear.
- Explore personal anecdotes or historical accounts where individuals reported heightened senses during fear.

Action Steps:
- Engage in mindfulness exercises to observe heightened sensations during fear.
- Experiment with controlled exposure to fear triggers to explore changes in sensory perception.

5. The Impact of Chronic Fear on Physical Health:

Overview:
- Examine the long-term consequences of chronic fear on physical health.
- Understand how sustained activation of the stress response can contribute to various health issues.

Exploration:
- Explore scientific literature on the connection between chronic stress, fear, and conditions like cardiovascular disease, immune system suppression, and digestive disorders.
- Investigate how chronic fear may manifest in psychosomatic symptoms.

Action Steps:
- Regularly assess and monitor your stress levels, especially if dealing with persistent fear.
- Consult with healthcare professionals to discuss strategies for managing chronic fear and its potential impact on physical health.

6. Mindful Body Scans and Progressive Relaxation:

Overview:
- Introduce the concept of mindful body scans and progressive relaxation as tools for recognizing and alleviating physical responses to fear.
- Explore how these practices promote awareness of tension and encourage relaxation.

Exploration:
- Investigate studies on the effectiveness of body scan meditations in reducing physiological arousal associated with fear.
- Explore the principles of progressive relaxation techniques and their impact on muscle tension.

Action Steps:
- Integrate mindful body scans into your daily routine to enhance awareness of physical sensations.
- Practice progressive relaxation before and after fear-inducing situations to observe changes in muscular tension.

7. Embodied Practices for Fear Management:

Overview:
- Explore embodied practices such as yoga, tai chi, or dance as holistic approaches to managing fear.
- Understand how these practices integrate physical movement with mindfulness and breath awareness.

Exploration:
- Investigate the physiological benefits of embodied practices for stress reduction and fear management.
- Explore different styles and philosophies of embodied practices to find a suitable fit for individual preferences.

Action Steps:

Diversify Learning Sources:
- Explore a variety of reputable sources, including books, academic articles, and documentaries, to gain a comprehensive understanding of fear's physiological aspects.
- Consider sources from neuroscience, psychology, and biology to get different perspectives.

Online Courses and Lectures:
- Enroll in online courses or attend lectures offered by experts in the field of neuroscience or psychology.
- Platforms like Coursera, edX, or academic institutions often offer courses that delve into the science behind fear.

Podcasts and Interviews:
- Listen to podcasts or interviews featuring experts in neuroscience or psychology discussing fear.
- Hearing discussions and real-world applications can complement formal learning and make the information more accessible.

Stay Informed on Latest Research:
- Regularly check reputable journals and publications for the latest research on fear and its physiological underpinnings.
- Stay informed about breakthroughs and evolving theories within the scientific community.

Chapter 4

Mapping Your Fears:
A Personal Fear Inventory

1. Understanding the Purpose of a Fear Inventory:
Overview:
- Recognize that a fear inventory is a tool for self-awareness and personal growth.
- Understand its role in identifying and categorizing fears to facilitate targeted exploration and intentional fear management.

Exploration:
- Research the benefits of creating a fear inventory in psychological literature and personal development resources.
- Reflect on how increased awareness of fears can contribute to a more empowered and fearless mindset.

Action Steps:

Reflect on Personal Growth Objectives:
- Consider your overarching goals for personal growth and development.
- Reflect on how understanding and navigating your fears aligns with these broader objectives.

Identify Specific Areas of Improvement:
- Break down your motivation into specific areas of life where you seek improvement.
- For example, you might be motivated to enhance relationships, boost confidence, or overcome specific challenges.

Explore the Desire for Emotional Resilience:
- Acknowledge the desire to cultivate emotional resilience and a more balanced mindset.
- Recognize that a fear inventory is a tool for building emotional intelligence and responding more effectively to life's challenges.

Consider the Impact on Well-Being:
- Contemplate how addressing fears contributes to overall well-being.
- Recognize that fearless living involves not just the absence of fear but a proactive and empowered response to fear-inducing situations.

Connect Motivation to Long-Term Vision:
- Align your motivation for the fear inventory with your long-term vision for a fulfilling and purpose-driven life.
- Consider how overcoming or navigating fears supports the realization of your aspirational goals.

2. Initiating the Fear Inventory Process:
Overview:
- Recognize that creating a fear inventory requires a systematic and introspective approach.
- Understand that fears may manifest in various aspects of life, including relationships, career, personal growth, and health.

Exploration:
- Explore different frameworks or models used in fear inventories, such as categorizing fears based on type, intensity, or impact.
- Consider how cultural, societal, and personal influences shape the perception of fears.

Action Steps:
- Set aside dedicated time for the fear inventory process, ensuring a calm and reflective environment.
- Begin with a mindset of curiosity and self-compassion, recognizing that fear is a universal human experience.

3. Identifying Categories and Types of Fears:
Overview:
- Recognize that fears can be categorized into different types, such as existential fears, social fears, or performance fears.
- Understand that exploring specific categories can provide insights into common themes and patterns.

Exploration:
- Reflect on your life experiences and identify recurring themes or situations that evoke fear.

- Consider utilizing psychological frameworks or models that classify fears based on their underlying nature.

Action Steps:
- Create categories that resonate with your experiences, ensuring they capture the diversity of your fears.
- List specific examples within each category to provide context and depth to your fear inventory.

4. Examining the Roots of Fear:
Overview:
- Acknowledge that fears often have roots in past experiences, beliefs, or conditioning.
- Understand that uncovering the origins of fear can provide valuable insights into their current impact.

Exploration:
- Engage in reflective exercises to trace the origins of specific fears in your life.
- Consider how societal expectations, family dynamics, or personal history contribute to the development of fears.

Action Steps:
- Approach the examination of fear roots with openness and non-judgment.
- Journal about significant life events or patterns that may have influenced the formation of specific fears.

5. Assessing the Impact of Fears on Daily Life:
Overview:
- Understand that fears can impact various aspects of your life, including decision-making, relationships, and overall well-being.
- Recognize that assessing the impact helps prioritize areas for focused attention and intervention.

Exploration:
- Reflect on how specific fears influence your behavior, choices, and overall quality of life.
- Consider seeking input from trusted friends, family, or mentors to gain an external perspective on the observable impact of your fears.

Action Steps:
- Create a comprehensive list of areas in your life where fears may be exerting an influence.
- Prioritize these areas based on their significance and your willingness to address them.

6. Rating Fear Intensity and Frequency:
Overview:
- Recognize that not all fears are equal in intensity or frequency.
- Understand that assigning ratings helps prioritize fears for targeted exploration and intervention.

Exploration:
- Reflect on the intensity of emotional responses during fear-inducing situations.
- Consider the frequency with which specific fears arise in different contexts.

Action Steps:
- Develop a rating system (e.g., on a scale of 1 to 10) to quantify the intensity and frequency of each fear.
- Use the ratings to identify high-priority fears that may require more immediate attention.

7. Creating a Fear Timeline:
Overview:
- Understand that fears often evolve and change over time.
- Recognize that creating a fear timeline provides a visual representation of the dynamic nature of fears in your life.

Exploration:
- Reflect on significant life events and their correlation with the emergence or transformation of specific fears.
- Consider using a visual format, such as a timeline or mind map, to illustrate the evolution of fears over different life stages.

Action Steps:
- Create a fear timeline that spans from childhood to the present, marking key events or transitions.
- Use the timeline to identify patterns, turning points, and the recurrence of specific fears.

8. Setting Fear Exploration Goals:
Overview:
- Recognize that the fear inventory process is a foundation for setting intentional exploration goals.

- Understand that establishing goals creates a roadmap for addressing fears and moving towards fearless living.

Exploration:
- Reflect on what you hope to achieve through the exploration of your fears.
- Consider framing goals in terms of personal growth, increased self-awareness, or specific fear mitigation strategies.

Action Steps:
- Set SMART goals (Specific, Measurable, Achievable, Relevant, Time-bound) related to fear exploration.
- Break down larger goals into smaller, manageable steps to create a structured approach.

9. Utilizing Support Systems:

Overview:
- Acknowledge that fear exploration can be a challenging and emotional process.
- Recognize the importance of seeking support from friends, family, or professionals during this journey.

Exploration:
- Identify individuals in your life whom you trust and feel comfortable sharing your fear inventory with.
- Consider the potential benefits of involving a mentor, coach, or therapist in your fear exploration process.

Action Steps:

Articulate Your Objectives Clearly:
- Clearly express your intentions behind undertaking a fear inventory to those you trust.
- Articulate the specific goals you aim to achieve through this process.

Share Your Motivation:
- Communicate the reasons driving your decision to explore and understand your fears.
- Share the broader context of personal growth, resilience-building, or specific areas of life improvement that motivate you.

Highlight the Positive Intent:
- Emphasize the positive intent behind the fear inventory, such as fostering self-awareness, improving decision-making, or enhancing emotional resilience.
- Clarify that your goal is not just to uncover fears but to develop adaptive responses to them.

Express Vulnerability:
- Share your vulnerability about the challenges you anticipate in the process.
- Express that you value their support in navigating this introspective journey.

Invite Input and Perspectives:
- Encourage open communication by inviting the input and perspectives of those you trust.
- Create a space for them to share their thoughts on the process and offer insights based on their own experiences.

Chapter 5

Historical Perspectives:
How Ancient Wisdom Addresses Fear

1. Acknowledging Ancient Wisdom:

Overview:
- Recognize the rich tapestry of ancient wisdom found in diverse cultures and philosophies.
- Understand that ancient civilizations cultivated profound insights into human psychology, resilience, and the nature of fear.

Exploration:
- Explore ancient texts, scriptures, and philosophical writings from cultures such as Greek, Roman, Chinese, Indian, and Egyptian.
- Recognize common themes and unique perspectives on fear embedded in these historical sources.

Action Steps:
- Create a curated reading list of ancient texts addressing fear.
- Develop a cross-cultural understanding of how different societies viewed and addressed fear.

2. Stoic Philosophy and Fear Resilience:

Overview:
- Delve into Stoic philosophy as a cornerstone of ancient wisdom addressing fear.
- Understand Stoic principles related to acceptance, control, and the cultivation of inner resilience.

Exploration:
- Study the works of Stoic philosophers such as Seneca, Epictetus, and Marcus Aurelius.
- Explore the Stoic concept of differentiating between what is within and beyond one's control.

Action Steps:
- Integrate negative visualization into your daily routine by setting aside a few moments for reflective contemplation.
- Focus on aspects of your life, relationships, or achievements, considering how they could be different or lost.
- Identify potential challenges or fears in your life that you can proactively premeditate.
- Visualize yourself navigating these challenges with Stoic principles in mind, fostering a sense of preparedness.
- When facing fear-inducing situations, consciously evaluate what aspects are within your control.
- Redirect your focus and energy towards actionable steps, fostering a sense of agency.

3. Buddhist Teachings on Fear and Attachment:

Overview:
- Explore Buddhist teachings that address the nature of fear and the role of attachment.
- Understand concepts such as impermanence, non-attachment, and mindfulness as tools for fear management.

Exploration:
- Study foundational Buddhist texts like the Dhammapada and the Four Noble Truths.
- Reflect on how the Eightfold Path provides practical guidance for alleviating suffering, including that caused by fear.

Action Steps:
- Dedicate a specific time each day for mindfulness meditation, creating a consistent routine.
- Start with short sessions and gradually extend the duration as you become more comfortable with the practice.
- Choose one or more daily activities to practice mindfulness intentionally.
- Pay attention to sensory experiences, thoughts, and emotions during these activities, cultivating a heightened awareness of the present moment.
- Incorporate mindfulness resources into your learning routine.
- Use guided meditations or readings to enhance your understanding and motivation for mindfulness practice.

4. **Ancient Chinese Philosophy and Harmony:**
Overview:
- Explore Chinese philosophies such as Confucianism, Taoism, and the I Ching for insights into harmony and balance.
- Understand how these philosophies emphasize alignment with the natural order to navigate fear.

Exploration:
- Read classical Chinese texts like the Analects of Confucius and the Tao Te Ching.
- Reflect on the concept of Wu Wei (effortless action) and its application in dealing with fear.

Action Steps:
- Before making decisions, practice a few moments of mindful breathing to center yourself.
- Consider the potential outcomes and emotional implications, aiming for decisions that align with a sense of balance, harmony, and inner calm.
- Choose a decision-making framework that aligns with the nature of the decision at hand.
- Systematically analyze factors like risks, benefits, and ethical considerations to promote a balanced and informed decision-making process.
- Before making significant decisions, consult with trusted advisors to gather diverse perspectives.
- Consider how their input aligns with your values and contributes to a more balanced understanding of the situation.

5. **Greco-Roman Philosophical Resilience:**
Overview:
- Examine Greco-Roman philosophical perspectives on cultivating resilience in the face of fear.
- Understand how concepts of virtue, reason, and self-discipline were central to addressing fear.

Exploration:
- Study works by philosophers like Aristotle, Epicurus, and the Stoics in the Greco-Roman tradition.
- Reflect on the emphasis placed on cultivating inner virtues as a means of facing fear with courage.

Action Steps:
- Identify key virtues that resonate with your values and aspirations.
- Before making decisions, consciously assess how each option aligns with the chosen virtues, fostering a sense of inner strength and ethical alignment.
- Set aside dedicated time for journaling, reflecting on daily experiences through the lens of virtue ethics.
- Periodically review past entries to observe patterns, celebrate virtuous achievements, and identify areas for growth.
- Before making significant decisions, pause to assess the ethical dimensions and implications.
- Consider the virtues relevant to the situation and prioritize choices that align with these virtues, fostering a sense of inner strength and ethical integrity.

6. **Indigenous Wisdom and Connection to Nature:**
Overview:
- Explore indigenous wisdom from various cultures, emphasizing the interconnectedness of humans and nature.
- Understand how a deep connection to the natural world can provide profound insights into fear and resilience.

Exploration:
- Investigate oral traditions, storytelling, and rituals from indigenous communities worldwide.
- Recognize the role of community, rituals, and the natural environment in addressing fear within these cultures.

Action Steps:
- Schedule regular forest bathing sessions, allowing for unhurried, mindful experiences in natural settings.
- Pay attention to sensory details during forest bathing, such as the rustling of leaves, bird sounds, and the scent of the forest, fostering a deep connection to nature.
- Incorporate nature walks into your routine, whether it's a daily stroll or a weekend hike.
- Experiment with different natural settings to discover the environments that resonate most with you.
- Dedicate specific times for outdoor meditation, choosing serene locations like parks, gardens, or natural reserves.
- Allow the sounds, sights, and sensations of nature to enhance your meditation experience, fostering a deeper connection to the environment.

7. Egyptian Wisdom and Symbolism:

Overview:

- Examine ancient Egyptian wisdom, mythology, and symbolism for insights into the human psyche and overcoming fear.
- Understand how symbolic representations and rituals played a role in addressing existential fears.

Exploration:

- Explore texts like the Egyptian Book of the Dead and hieroglyphic symbolism.
- Consider the significance of rituals such as mummification and burial practices in addressing the fear of death.

Action Steps:

- Design a ritual that involves specific actions, symbols, or ceremonies representing your commitment to transcending fear.
- Regularly engage in this ritual during significant milestones or when facing fear-inducing situations, reinforcing a sense of empowerment and courage.
- Carry the symbolic object with you as a daily companion, especially during situations that evoke fear.
- Develop a ritual around the object, such as holding or touching it during moments of reflection or before facing challenges, reinforcing the symbolism of courage.
- Plan and organize a personal or community ceremony that marks the triumph over fear.
- Incorporate symbolic elements, such as fire, water, or ceremonial objects, to represent the transformative nature of the fear-transcendence journey.

Chapter 6

The Science of Fear:
Insights from Neuroscience

Neurobiological Basis of Fear:
1.Amygdala's Role in Fear Processing:
Overview:
- Delve into the amygdala's central role in processing and regulating fear responses.
- Recognize the amygdala's connection to emotional memory and its influence on decision-making.

Exploration:
- Explore scientific studies and literature on the amygdala's function in fear conditioning.
- Reflect on how the amygdala's activation contributes to the immediate emotional response to fear-inducing stimuli.

Action Steps:
- Regularly review your reflections to discern patterns in emotional reactions.
- Develop a heightened sensitivity to potential triggers by staying attuned to both external and internal cues.
- Integrate brief body scan exercises into your daily routine, especially during moments of heightened stress or unease.
- Use the information gathered to pinpoint physiological signs that accompany emotional reactions, contributing to proactive awareness.
- During moments of emotional intensity, take a step back mentally and observe the emotions without getting entangled in the narrative.
- Refrain from self-criticism and instead focus on understanding the emotions as transient and informative signals.

2.Neurotransmitters and Fear Modulation:
Overview:
- Examine the role of neurotransmitters, such as serotonin and dopamine, in modulating fear responses.
- Understand how imbalances in neurotransmitter levels can contribute to anxiety and fear-related disorders.

Exploration:
- Explore neuroscience research on the impact of neurotransmitters on mood regulation and fear processing.
- Reflect on how lifestyle factors, including diet and exercise, influence neurotransmitter levels.

Action Steps:
- Incorporate brief mindful breathing sessions into your daily routine, especially during moments of stress or tension.
- Use breath awareness as a tool to connect with the present and observe emotional reactions without immediate judgment.
- Dedicate time to regular body scan meditations, focusing on each part of the body and acknowledging any emotional or physical sensations.
- Use the body scan as a tool to cultivate a non-judgmental awareness of the mind-body connection.
- Set aside dedicated time for journaling, making it a consistent part of your daily or weekly routine.
- Use journal entries as a tool to identify moments when the amygdala might be activated, fostering a deeper understanding of emotional responses.
- Rewiring the Brain for Fearlessness:

1.Neuroplasticity and Fear Conditioning:
Overview:
- Investigate the concept of neuroplasticity and its role in rewiring the brain's responses to fear.
- Understand how repeated exposure to fear-inducing stimuli shapes neural pathways.

Exploration:

- Explore neuroscientific studies on the adaptability of the brain in response to experiences and environmental stimuli.
- Reflect on how fear conditioning contributes to the formation of neural circuits associated with fear.

Action Steps:

- Begin exposure with the least anxiety-provoking fear trigger from the hierarchy.
- Gradually progress through the hierarchy, exposing yourself to increasingly challenging situations as you build resilience.
- Practice controlled exposure by exposing yourself to a fear trigger for a short duration initially.
- Gradually increase the duration and intensity of exposure, always prioritizing self-care and seeking support if needed.

2.Mindfulness and Fear Modulation:

Overview:

- Explore how mindfulness practices impact brain regions associated with fear, such as the prefrontal cortex.
- Recognize the role of mindfulness in promoting emotional regulation and reducing amygdala activation.

Exploration:

- Examine neuroscientific studies on the effects of mindfulness meditation on brain structure and function.
- Reflect on the correlation between increased prefrontal cortex activity and improved emotional regulation.

Action Steps:

- Designate a specific area in your home or choose a quiet outdoor space for meditation.
- Personalize the space with calming elements like cushions, candles, or soothing colors to enhance the meditative atmosphere.
- Schedule mindfulness meditation sessions at the same time each day, fostering a sense of routine.
- Experiment with different time slots to find the one that feels most conducive to a focused and uninterrupted practice.
- Initiate your mindfulness meditation practice with sessions as short as 5-10 minutes.
- Gradually extend the duration as you become more comfortable and attuned to the practice.
- Practical Applications for Fearless Living:

1.Neuroscience-Informed Fear Exposure:

Overview:

- Explore systematic desensitization techniques rooted in neuroscience to confront and overcome specific fears.
- Understand the principles of gradual fear exposure for fear extinction.

Exploration:

- Review studies on exposure therapy and its effectiveness in reshaping neural pathways associated with fear.
- Reflect on personalized fear exposure plans tailored to individual fears and triggers.

Action Steps:

- Develop a fear hierarchy, ranking fears from least to most challenging, and systematically expose yourself to these situations.
- Track progress and celebrate achievements to reinforce positive neural adaptations.

2.Neurofeedback for Fear Modulation:

Overview:

- Investigate neurofeedback as a therapeutic approach to train the brain in real-time to regulate fear responses.
- Understand how neurofeedback enhances self-regulation by providing individuals with real-time information about their brain activity.

Exploration:

- Explore neuroscientific studies on the efficacy of neurofeedback in treating anxiety and fear-related disorders.
- Reflect on how individuals can learn to self-regulate brain activity associated with fear.

Action Steps:
- Consult with trained professionals to explore neurofeedback as a complementary approach to fear management.
- Practice neurofeedback exercises with guidance to enhance self-awareness and improve fear modulation.
- Integration of Neuroscience and Fearless Living:

1.Educational Resources on Neuroscience of Fear:

Overview:
- Curate a list of reputable educational resources, books, and documentaries explaining the neuroscience of fear.
- Understand the value of ongoing learning in integrating neuroscience principles into fearless living.

Exploration:
- Explore online courses, scientific journals, and popular science literature on the neuroscience of fear.
- Reflect on how a deeper understanding of neuroscience can empower individuals to navigate fear more effectively.

Action Steps:
- Dedicate time to learning about the neuroscience of fear from credible sources.
- Share relevant resources with others to create a culture of informed fear management.

2.Neuroscience-Informed Fear Resilience Training:

Overview:
- Develop a personalized fear resilience training program informed by neuroscience principles.
- Recognize the importance of ongoing practice in reinforcing neuroplastic changes.

Exploration:
- Explore interdisciplinary approaches that combine neuroscience, psychology, and mindfulness in fear resilience training.
- Reflect on how consistent practice contributes to lasting changes in neural pathways associated with fear.

Action Steps:
- Create a categorized list of fear triggers, distinguishing between situational, cognitive, and emotional aspects.
- Prioritize fear triggers based on perceived intensity and relevance, providing a foundation for targeted resilience training.

Chapter 7

Fear in the Digital Age:
Navigating Modern Anxieties

1. Understanding Digital Anxieties:
Overview:
- Recognize the unique challenges and anxieties that arise in the digital age, including but not limited to social media, information overload, cyber threats, and digital comparison.
- Understand the impact of constant connectivity on mental health and well-being.

Exploration:
- Explore the ways in which digital technologies contribute to the amplification of fears and anxieties.
- Reflect on personal experiences with digital anxieties, considering the role of social media, online information consumption, and digital interactions.

Action Steps:
- Create a structured checklist for the digital audit, encompassing social media habits, online content consumption, and communication channels.
- Use digital tracking tools or apps to monitor the time spent on various digital activities.
- Maintain a digital journal to record emotional states before and after engaging in various online activities.
- Consider seeking feedback from close friends or family about observed changes in your mood or behavior related to digital interactions.
- Develop a list of positive aspects of digital engagement that align with your values and goals.
- Create strategies to mitigate the negative impact, such as setting time limits, unfollowing triggering content, or implementing digital detox days.

2.Managing Social Media Anxiety:
Overview:
- Recognize the potential for social media to contribute to anxiety through comparison, cyberbullying, and the pressure to curate a perfect online image.
- Understand the importance of setting healthy boundaries with social media use.

Exploration:
- Explore the phenomenon of social comparison and its impact on self-esteem and fear of missing out (FOMO).
- Reflect on personal social media habits and their connection to emotional well-being.

Action Steps:
- Establish a defined period for the social media detox, ranging from a few days to a few weeks.
- Disable notifications to reduce the temptation to check social media during the detox period.
- Define specific time limits for daily social media use, considering both overall duration and specific time slots.
- Designate social media-free periods, such as during meals, before bedtime, or on certain days of the week.
- Implement strategies to reduce constant connectivity, such as turning off non-essential notifications or using dedicated apps to monitor screen time.
- Create physical barriers, such as placing the phone in another room during designated social media-free periods.

3.Building Digital Literacy:
Overview:
- Recognize the role of misinformation, online scams, and cyber threats in contributing to digital anxieties.
- Understand the importance of developing critical thinking skills in the digital landscape.

Exploration:
- Explore common tactics used in online misinformation and phishing scams.
- Reflect on personal experiences with encountering false information online and the emotional impact.

Action Steps:
- Research reputable online courses, workshops, or educational platforms that offer comprehensive digital literacy training.
- Allocate dedicated time in your schedule for continuous learning and skill development.
- Familiarize yourself with reputable fact-checking websites and tools available for verifying information.
- Cultivate a habit of fact-checking before sharing any information, especially if it has the potential to influence others.
- Develop a checklist or mental framework for evaluating the credibility of online sources.
- Prioritize information from authoritative sources, academic institutions, and recognized experts.

4.Cultivating Mindful Digital Consumption:

Overview:
- Recognize the impact of constant digital consumption on mental health, including information overload and digital burnout.
- Understand the benefits of mindful digital consumption for overall well-being.

Exploration:
- Explore the concept of digital mindfulness and its application in managing anxiety.
- Reflect on the relationship between digital consumption patterns and stress levels.

Action Steps:
- Create a digital usage schedule, designating specific times for checking emails, social media, and other digital activities.
- Experiment with mindfulness apps that encourage brief meditation or breathing exercises to center yourself during digital interactions.
- Establish criteria for evaluating the quality of digital content, considering factors such as relevance, reliability, and authenticity.
- Curate your digital feeds by unfollowing accounts or sources that do not contribute positively to your well-being.
- Identify and declutter digital spaces, such as your social media feeds, email subscriptions, and digital workspace.
- Consider implementing digital detox days or weekends where you intentionally disconnect from digital devices.

5.Establishing Healthy Online Relationships:

Overview:
- Recognize the impact of online interactions on emotional well-being, including the potential for cyberbullying, online harassment, and the importance of positive connections.
- Understand the role of digital communication in fostering or hindering meaningful relationships.

Exploration:
- Explore the potential challenges of maintaining healthy boundaries and communication in online relationships.
- Reflect on personal experiences with positive and negative online interactions.

Action Steps:
- Regularly assess your social media connections, unfollowing or muting individuals or pages that consistently share content that is distressing or conflicts with your values.
- Consider creating separate lists or groups to categorize connections based on their positive or negative impact.
- Actively participate in discussions, share positive content, and contribute to creating a supportive atmosphere within your chosen online communities.
- Seek out new groups or forums that align with your interests and encourage positive interactions.
- Clearly define and communicate your digital boundaries to friends, family, and online connections.
- Set specific time limits for daily digital use and establish designated periods for digital detox.

6.Cybersecurity and Personal Safety:

Overview:
- Recognize the fear associated with online threats, including identity theft, hacking, and the compromise of personal information.
- Understand the importance of adopting cybersecurity measures for personal safety.

Exploration:
- Explore common cybersecurity threats and methods employed by cybercriminals.

- Reflect on personal cybersecurity practices and potential vulnerabilities.

Action Steps:
- Implement strong and unique passwords for all online accounts, utilizing a combination of uppercase letters, lowercase letters, numbers, and symbols.
- Enable two-factor authentication (2FA) whenever available, adding an extra layer of security to your accounts.
- Subscribe to newsletters or updates from cybersecurity organizations to receive timely information about emerging threats.
- Set aside dedicated time for regular reading and education on cybersecurity trends.
- Dedicate time for ongoing education on cybersecurity best practices, covering topics such as secure browsing, safe online shopping, and protection against social engineering attacks.
- Seek certifications or credentials in cybersecurity if relevant to your personal or professional goals.

7.Balancing Digital Engagement and Real-world Connection:

Overview:
- Recognize the importance of balancing digital engagement with real-world connections for holistic well-being.
- Understand the potential for digital isolation and the impact on mental health.

Exploration:
- Explore the concept of digital minimalism and its benefits in fostering genuine human connections.
- Reflect on personal experiences with finding a healthy balance between online and offline relationships.

Action Steps:
- Establish a weekly schedule that includes dedicated periods of unplugged time.
- Communicate your commitment to unplugged intervals with friends and family to manage expectations.
- Set clear intentions before engaging in digital activities, outlining the purpose and duration.
- Implement conscious breaks during digital use to check in on your emotional state and adjust engagement accordingly.
- Schedule regular face-to-face interactions with friends, family, or community members.
- Engage in activities that foster genuine connections, such as shared hobbies, events, or volunteering.

Chapter **8**

The Fear-Love Dichotomy:
Balancing Emotional Polarities

1. Mindful Integration
Overview:
- Recognize the coexistence of fear and love as integral aspects of the human experience.
- Understand the importance of acknowledging both emotions for a harmonious emotional landscape.
- Cultivate mindfulness to consciously integrate the awareness of fear and love in daily life.
- Embrace the idea that a balanced emotional state contributes to overall well-being.
- Explore activities that invite the simultaneous presence of fear and love, fostering a mindful balance.

Exploration:
- Reflect on personal experiences where fear and love intersect, observing the emotional nuances.
- Identify instances where acknowledging both fear and love enhanced your emotional experience.
- Dive into the origins of fear and love in various aspects of your life, seeking a deeper understanding.
- Explore cultural or societal influences that may impact the perception of these emotions.
- Journal about moments where a lack of mindful integration led to imbalances in emotional responses.

Action Steps:
- ✓ Expand Duration Gradually: Start with a few minutes each day and gradually increase the duration of your mindfulness practice.
- ✓ Incorporate Breath Awareness: Focus on your breath, using it as an anchor to bring your attention to the present moment.
- ✓ Mindful Check-ins: Integrate short mindful check-ins throughout the day, cultivating awareness of your emotional state.
- ✓ Identify Personal Triggers: Reflect on activities that evoke both fear and love, tailoring the list to your unique emotional landscape.
- ✓ Variety in Experiences: Include a diverse range of activities, from outdoor adventures to creative pursuits, ensuring a holistic approach.
- ✓ Scheduled Integration: Allocate specific times for these activities, creating intentional moments for emotional exploration.
- ✓ Select a Trusted Companion: Choose a friend, mentor, or family member with whom you feel comfortable sharing your emotional journey.
- ✓ Regular Check-ins: Schedule periodic check-ins to discuss insights, challenges, and victories related to mindful integration.

Reciprocal Sharing: Encourage open dialogue, allowing for reciprocal sharing of experiences and perspectives.

2.Journaling for Authenticity
- ✓ **Overview:**
- ✓ Emphasize the role of journaling in expressing genuine emotions without judgment.
- ✓ Recognize journaling as a tool for gaining insights into emotional patterns and triggers.
- ✓ Establish a routine for reflective journaling to encourage authentic self-expression.
- ✓ Understand the therapeutic benefits of exploring both positive and challenging emotions.
- ✓ Link the practice of authentic journaling to increased self-awareness and emotional intelligence.

Exploration:
- ✓ Review past journal entries to identify recurring patterns in fear and love expressions.
- ✓ Experiment with various journaling prompts that encourage exploration of both emotions.
- ✓ Consider how external influences shape your journaling, affecting the authenticity of your expressions.
- ✓ Explore different journaling styles (artistic, narrative, or gratitude-focused) to find what resonates best.
- ✓ Reflect on moments where journaling facilitated a deeper understanding of your emotional landscape.

Action Steps:
- ✓ Establish a consistent journaling routine, dedicating time each day or week for authentic expression.
- ✓ Experiment with multimedia journaling, incorporating images, drawings, or collages to enhance self-expression.

- ✓ Share selected journal entries with a trusted friend or therapist, promoting open communication.
- ✓ Attend journaling workshops or join online communities to gain new perspectives and techniques.
- ✓ Compile a list of journaling prompts that specifically target the exploration of fear and love.
- ✓ Define clear emotional boundaries with specific triggers or influences that disrupt balance.
- ✓ Communicate your emotional boundaries with close relationships, fostering understanding and support.
- ✓ Designate specific times or spaces where you consciously limit exposure to external emotional triggers.
- ✓ Seek professional guidance, such as therapy or counseling, to explore and establish healthy emotional boundaries.
- ✓ Join support groups or communities that promote the importance of intentional emotional boundaries.
- ✓ Identify specific fear-facing strategies that resonate with you and incorporate them into your routine.
- ✓ Explore love-embracing practices that contribute to emotional resilience, such as gratitude or compassion exercises.
- ✓ Develop a resilient toolbox that includes a variety of strategies for different fear and love scenarios.
- ✓ Engage in activities that challenge your comfort zones, contributing to the development of emotional resilience.
- ✓ Attend resilience workshops or courses to deepen your understanding and application of resilience-building techniques.

3.Setting Emotional Boundaries

Overview:
- ✓ Emphasize the significance of establishing emotional boundaries for a balanced emotional state.
- ✓ Recognize the impact of external influences on emotional well-being and the fear-love dynamic.
- ✓ Understand that intentional emotional boundaries contribute to a more conscious emotional experience.
- ✓ Link emotional boundaries to resilience and the ability to navigate various emotional states effectively.
- ✓ Explore the concept of limiting exposure to media or societal expectations to maintain emotional balance.

Exploration:
- ✓ Identify specific external influences that tend to disrupt the balance between fear and love.
- ✓ Reflect on instances where setting emotional boundaries positively impacted your emotional well-being.
- ✓ Explore how societal expectations contribute to the fear-love dynamic, examining cultural influences.
- ✓ Consider the role of emotional boundaries in interpersonal relationships and self-care practices.
- ✓ Examine the potential consequences of lacking emotional boundaries on overall emotional resilience.

Action Steps:
- ✓ Self-Reflection: Engage in deep self-reflection to identify specific triggers or influences that disrupt emotional balance.
- ✓ Articulate Boundaries: Clearly define and articulate emotional boundaries, making them explicit for personal clarity.
- ✓ Honest Dialogue: Initiate honest and open conversations with close relationships about your emotional boundaries.
- ✓ Share Personal Insights: Communicate your self-reflections and insights, fostering mutual understanding.
- ✓ Create Safe Spaces: Designate specific physical spaces where you can retreat and focus on emotional well-being.
- ✓ Time Block Strategies: Schedule specific times in your routine to consciously limit exposure to external emotional triggers.
- ✓ Incorporate Rituals: Develop rituals around these designated times or spaces, reinforcing the intentional nature of emotional boundaries.

4. Building Fear-Love Resilience

Overview:
- ✓ Highlight the connection between resilience and the ability to navigate both fear and love.
- ✓ Recognize resilience-building as a dynamic process that incorporates elements of fear-facing and love-embracing approaches.
- ✓ Understand that a resilient mindset contributes to personal growth and emotional well-being.

- ✓ Emphasize the role of a resilient toolbox in effectively managing challenges arising from fear and love.
- ✓ Explore the idea that resilience involves adapting to and learning from both positive and challenging experiences.

Exploration:
- ✓ Reflect on past challenges where resilience played a crucial role in overcoming fear or embracing love.
- ✓ Explore cultural or personal narratives that emphasize resilience in the face of adversity.
- ✓ Consider how fear and love can act as catalysts for resilience, fostering adaptability and strength.
- ✓ Examine your current resilience strategies and identify areas for improvement.
- ✓ Delve into stories of individuals who have successfully navigated the fear-love dichotomy, gaining inspiration for building resilience.

Action Steps:
- ✓ **Self-Discovery:** Reflect on past experiences to identify strategies that have effectively helped you face fear.
- ✓ **Experiment with Techniques:** Explore a range of fear-facing techniques, from visualization to exposure therapy, to find what resonates.
- ✓ **Incorporate into Routine:** Integrate chosen strategies into your daily routine, ensuring consistent practice.
- ✓ **Gratitude Exercises:** Cultivate a habit of expressing gratitude, either through journaling or daily reflections.
- ✓ **Compassion Building:** Engage in exercises that promote compassion, fostering a positive and loving mindset.
- ✓ **Random Acts of Kindness:** Integrate acts of kindness into your routine, contributing to a more love-centric perspective.
- ✓ **Diverse Strategies:** Include a variety of fear-facing and love-embracing strategies in your toolbox.
- ✓ **Adaptability:** Ensure your toolbox is adaptable, with strategies suitable for different intensities and types of fear and love.
- ✓ **Regular Review:** Periodically assess and update your toolbox based on personal growth and evolving emotional needs.
- ✓ **Regularly Seek Discomfort:** Actively look for opportunities that challenge your comfort zones, fostering emotional resilience.
- ✓ **Incremental Progress:** Start with small challenges and gradually increase the level of discomfort to build resilience over time.
- ✓ **Reflect on Growth:** Regularly reflect on your emotional journey, acknowledging and celebrating progress in facing fears.

Chapter 9

Breaking Down Phobias:
Strategies for Specific Fears

1. Fear of Public Speaking
Overview:
- Public speaking anxiety is a common fear, impacting personal and professional development. Overcoming this fear involves targeted strategies to build confidence and effective communication skills.

Exploration:
- Reflect on past public speaking experiences, identifying specific triggers.
- Examine the root causes of anxiety, whether it's fear of judgment, criticism, or performance anxiety.

Action Steps:
- Start with small, comfortable speaking engagements and progressively increase audience size.
- Record and review your speeches for self-assessment.
- Enroll in public speaking courses or workshops to enhance communication techniques.
- Practice articulation and body language in front of a mirror.
- Visualize successful speaking experiences, focusing on confident and positive outcomes.
- Replace negative thoughts with affirmations before and during speeches.
- Seek constructive feedback from peers, mentors, or speech coaches.
- Use feedback to make targeted improvements in subsequent presentations.
- Participate in public speaking clubs or groups to gain exposure and support.
- Engage in impromptu speaking exercises to build spontaneity.
- Incorporate mindfulness practices to manage anxiety and stay present during speeches.
- Practice deep breathing exercises to calm nerves before speaking engagements.
- Embrace authenticity and genuine connection with the audience.

2. Fear of Heights
Overview:
- Acrophobia, or the fear of heights, can limit various life experiences. Overcoming this fear involves gradual exposure, understanding triggers, and building a sense of control.

Exploration:
- Explore the origins of the fear, considering past experiences or traumas related to heights.
- Identify specific scenarios triggering heightened anxiety, whether it's looking down from heights or standing on elevated surfaces.

Action Steps:
- Create a hierarchy of height exposures, starting with less intimidating scenarios.
- Gradually progress to more challenging situations as confidence grows.
- Engage in virtual reality exposure therapy to simulate height scenarios.
- Gradually transition to real-life exposure as comfort increases.
- Learn about the physics of heights and safety measures in place.
- Attend workshops or lectures on overcoming the fear of heights.
- Consider cognitive-behavioral therapy (CBT) with a focus on systematic desensitization.
- Work with a therapist to explore the underlying causes and coping mechanisms.
- Practice grounding exercises like toe tapping or gripping an object to stay connected to the ground.
- Use physical anchors to create a sense of stability.
- Use guided imagery exercises to visualize positive experiences at heights.
- Gradually introduce more challenging imagery as tolerance increases.
- Engage in height-related activities with a supportive friend or family member.
- Share fears and progress, fostering a sense of shared accomplishment.
- Acknowledge and celebrate reaching specific height-related milestones.
- Reinforce positive associations with elevated spaces.

3. Fear of Flying
Overview:
- Aerophobia, or the fear of flying, can hinder travel and limit personal experiences. Overcoming this fear involves understanding aviation, addressing specific triggers, and implementing coping strategies.

Exploration:
- Identify specific aspects of flying that trigger anxiety, such as turbulence or claustrophobia.
- Reflect on any past negative experiences related to air travel.

Action Steps:
- Attend aviation courses or workshops to understand the mechanics and safety of flying.
- Gain knowledge about turbulence, safety measures, and the role of pilots.
- Begin with visits to airports without the pressure of boarding a flight.
- Familiarize yourself with airport layouts and procedures.
- Practice positive visualization of successful and calm flight experiences.
- Gradually incorporate more details, such as boarding and takeoff.
- Engage in relaxation exercises before boarding, such as deep breathing or progressive muscle relaxation.
- Develop a pre-flight routine to create a sense of familiarity.
- Travel with a supportive friend or family member.
- Communicate openly about fears and seek reassurance during the journey.
- Enroll in fear-of-flying programs or workshops offered by airlines or mental health professionals.
- Benefit from guided exposure and support from experienced professionals.
- Prepare a distraction toolkit, including books, movies, or music, to occupy your mind during flights.
- Use noise-canceling headphones to minimize anxiety-inducing sounds.
- Practice mindfulness techniques during turbulence, focusing on the present moment.
- Join online forums or communities for individuals with a fear of flying.
- Share experiences, strategies, and encouragement with others facing similar challenges.

4. Fear of Failure
Overview:
- A pervasive fear, aversion to failure can hinder personal and professional growth. Overcoming this fear involves reframing perspectives, setting realistic goals, and building resilience.

Exploration:
- Explore the origins of the fear of failure, considering past experiences or societal expectations.
- Identify specific situations or endeavors where the fear of failure is most prominent.

Action Steps:
- Embrace failure as a natural part of the learning process.
- View failures as opportunities for growth and refinement.
- Break down larger goals into smaller, manageable tasks.
- Celebrate small victories along the way, reinforcing progress.
- Cultivate positive self-talk to counteract negative beliefs.
- Develop affirmations that reinforce confidence and resilience.
- Analyze failures as feedback, identifying areas for improvement.
- Implement lessons learned from failures into future endeavors.
- Visualize success even in the face of challenges.
- Create mental images of overcoming obstacles and achieving goals.
- Embrace imperfection as a natural part of the human experience.
- Avoid perfectionist tendencies that intensify the fear of failure.
- Connect with mentors who have experienced failure and achieved success.
- Seek guidance on navigating challenges and setbacks.
- Study the lives of successful individuals, acknowledging their struggles and failures.
- Shift focus from solely celebrating successful outcomes to acknowledging effort.
- Recognize the value of perseverance and resilience in the face of challenges.
- Channel energy into skill development rather than fear of failure.
- Recognize that improvement is a continuous process.

5. Fear of Rejection

Overview:

- The fear of rejection can impact personal relationships and hinder social interactions. Overcoming this fear involves building self-confidence, understanding rejection as subjective, and developing effective communication skills.

Exploration:

- Reflect on past experiences of rejection and their impact on self-esteem.
- Identify specific situations or interactions where the fear of rejection is most pronounced.

Action Steps:

- Engage in activities that boost self-esteem and confidence.
- Surround yourself with positive influences that uplift and support.
- Recognize that rejection is often subjective and influenced by various factors.
- Understand that rejection doesn't define personal worth.
- Develop assertiveness and effective communication skills.
- Express thoughts and feelings clearly, reducing misinterpretation.
- Embrace the impermanence of relationships and interactions.
- Understand that not every connection will lead to long-lasting bonds.
- Begin with low-stakes social interactions and progressively increase exposure.
- Gradually face situations that trigger the fear of rejection.
- Visualize successful social interactions, focusing on positive outcomes.
- Replace negative anticipations with optimistic scenarios.

Chapter 10

Fear's Illusions:
Distinguishing Real vs. Perceived Threats

1. Analyzing Past Experiences
Overview:
- Recognize the impact of past experiences on shaping perceptions of threats and the subsequent influence on fear responses.

Exploration:
- Reflect on specific incidents from your past where fear played a significant role.
- Identify the emotions associated with these experiences and their lasting effects.
- Examine how fear from past events may be influencing your current perception of threats.
- Consider the role of cognitive biases in shaping your interpretation of past events.
- Assess whether the fear experienced in the past was proportionate to the actual threat.

Action Steps:
- Create a chronological timeline of significant fear-inducing events in your life.
- Journal about the emotions and thought patterns linked to each event.
- Engage in therapy or counseling to gain professional insights into the impact of past experiences.
- Implement mindfulness practices to observe and detach from emotional responses tied to past fears.
- Gradually expose yourself to situations reminiscent of past fears, assessing your current reactions.
- Seek feedback from trusted individuals who witnessed or were involved in the past events.
- Challenge distorted memories through cognitive restructuring techniques.
- Establish positive associations with past fear-inducing situations through guided visualization.
- Share your reflections on past fears with a supportive friend or mentor.
- Celebrate instances where you've successfully overcome the lingering effects of past fears.

2. Investigating Cognitive Patterns
Overview:
- Explore the role of cognitive processes in shaping the perception of threats, leading to the formation of fear-based responses.

Exploration:
- Analyze thought patterns during fear-inducing situations, focusing on automatic cognitive responses.
- Recognize cognitive distortions, such as catastrophizing or black-and-white thinking, associated with perceived threats.
- Explore the influence of core beliefs and schemas on the interpretation of potential dangers.
- Examine the connection between cognitive patterns and emotional reactions during fear.
- Understand the impact of cognitive biases, such as confirmation bias, in reinforcing perceived threats.

Action Steps:
- Engage in mindfulness practices to observe automatic thoughts without judgment.
- Keep a thought journal during fear-inducing situations to identify recurring cognitive patterns.
- Attend cognitive-behavioral therapy (CBT) sessions to address and challenge cognitive distortions.
- Use cognitive restructuring techniques to replace irrational thoughts with more balanced interpretations.
- Develop a list of positive affirmations that counteract fear-based cognitive patterns.
- Seek feedback from others on your thought processes during fear-inducing situations.
- Participate in cognitive training programs to enhance cognitive flexibility.
- Utilize visualization exercises to rehearse calm and rational thought responses.
- Join support groups that focus on addressing and changing maladaptive cognitive patterns.
- Collaborate with a mental health professional to create personalized strategies for cognitive restructuring.

3. Unmasking Fear-Driven Behaviors
Overview:

- Explore the behavioral manifestations of fear and understand how certain actions may be driven by perceived threats.

Exploration:
- Identify behaviors that are consistently associated with fear or anxiety.
- Examine patterns of avoidance or procrastination as potential indicators of fear-based responses.
- Analyze the impact of fear on decision-making processes and behavioral choices.
- Consider how perfectionism may be linked to an underlying fear of failure or judgment.
- Reflect on instances where fear has influenced your interpersonal relationships and interactions.

Action Steps:
- Keep a behavior journal to track actions correlated with fear or anxiety.
- Gradually expose yourself to fear-inducing situations to observe and manage behavioral responses.
- Set small, achievable goals in areas where fear-driven behaviors are prominent.
- Seek feedback from trusted individuals on how your behaviors may be influenced by fear.
- Engage in cognitive-behavioral therapy (CBT) to address and modify fear-driven behaviors.
- Implement systematic desensitization techniques to reduce avoidance behaviors.
- Utilize positive reinforcement to reward and encourage fear-resistant behaviors.
- Collaborate with a mentor or coach to develop strategies for breaking fear-driven habits.
- Join support groups focused on behavioral change and overcoming specific fears.
- Practice self-compassion to foster a positive mindset during periods of fear-driven behaviors.

4. The Role of Fear in Decision-Making

Overview:
- Examine how fear can influence decision-making processes and contribute to a reluctance to take risks.

Exploration:
- Reflect on past decisions made under the influence of fear and their outcomes.
- Identify decision-making patterns associated with risk aversion or a fear of failure.
- Explore the connection between fear and the tendency to seek certainty in decision-making.
- Analyze the impact of fear on the ability to embrace change and adaptability.
- Consider how fear may lead to decisions aligned with short-term comfort rather than long-term goals.

Action Steps:
- Develop a decision-making journal to document the emotions and factors influencing each decision.
- Engage in mindfulness practices to observe and detach from fear-based influences on decision-making.
- Set intentional goals that challenge the need for certainty in decision processes.
- Consult with a decision coach or mentor to gain alternative perspectives on fearful decision-making.
- Practice making small decisions in the face of uncertainty to build tolerance for ambiguity.
- Utilize decision-making frameworks to objectively evaluate choices independent of fear.
- Attend decision-making workshops or seminars to enhance skills in overcoming fear-driven decisions.
- Seek out diverse opinions and feedback before making decisions influenced by fear.
- Embrace a growth mindset, viewing mistakes and failures as opportunities for learning and growth.
- Gradually expose yourself to decision-making situations that trigger fear, building resilience over time.

5. Fear's Influence on Interpersonal Relationships

Overview:
- Examine how fear can impact the quality of interpersonal connections and overall relationship dynamics.

Exploration:
- Reflect on past relationship patterns influenced by fear, including attachment styles.
- Identify communication challenges and conflicts rooted in fear-based responses.
- Analyze the role of fear in forming and maintaining interpersonal boundaries.
- Explore how fear may contribute to a fear of vulnerability or intimacy in relationships.
- Reflect on the impact of fear on social interactions, including meeting new people or networking.

Action Steps:
- Attend relationship workshops or therapy sessions to explore and address fear-related patterns.
- Practice active listening and assertiveness to enhance communication skills within relationships.
- Engage in vulnerability exercises to build resilience in sharing emotions and thoughts.

- Set clear and healthy boundaries in relationships, communicating them openly.
- Seek relationship coaching or counseling to navigate fear-driven challenges.
- Participate in social activities to gradually expose yourself to fear-inducing social situations.
- Develop a support network to discuss and process fears related to interpersonal relationships.
- Utilize self-reflection and journaling to identify and address fear-driven relationship patterns.
- Join community groups or clubs to expand social connections and challenge fear.
- Foster empathy in relationships, recognizing and understanding the fears of others.

Chapter 11

The Art of Exposure:
Gradual Desensitization Techniques

1: Understanding the Significance of Exposure
Overview:
- Recognize the importance of exposure as a therapeutic technique for overcoming fears and phobias.

Exploration:
- Investigate the historical and psychological foundations of exposure therapy.
- Explore case studies or success stories where exposure has been effective in fear reduction.
- Understand the neuroscience behind exposure and how it impacts the brain's fear response.
- Reflect on personal experiences where exposure has played a role in fear reduction.
- Examine potential misconceptions or concerns about exposure therapy.

Action Steps:
- Research reputable sources, books, or articles on exposure therapy to gain foundational knowledge.
- Consult with mental health professionals or therapists experienced in exposure techniques.
- Identify and list specific fears or phobias you wish to address through exposure.
- Set clear and realistic goals for the desired outcomes of exposure therapy.
- Discuss your interest in exposure with a mental health professional for personalized insights.
- Create a support system with friends or family members aware of your exposure journey.
- Develop a hierarchy of fear-inducing situations, starting with the least distressing.
- Gradually expose yourself to low-level fear scenarios to build tolerance.
- Use mindfulness techniques during exposure to observe and manage emotional responses.
- Journal your experiences, noting progress, challenges, and any shifts in fear perceptions.

2: Unveiling the Power of Systematic Desensitization
Overview:
- Understand the systematic desensitization process as a structured approach to reducing fear and anxiety.

Exploration:
- Explore the roots of systematic desensitization in behavior therapy.
- Understand how systematic desensitization targets the learned fear response.
- Investigate the principles of reciprocal inhibition and how they relate to desensitization.
- Reflect on real-life scenarios where systematic desensitization has been successfully applied.
- Consider the role of relaxation techniques within systematic desensitization.

Action Steps:
- Learn and practice relaxation techniques, such as deep breathing or progressive muscle relaxation.
- Create a personalized hierarchy of fear-inducing situations for systematic desensitization.
- Gradually expose yourself to feared scenarios while maintaining a relaxed state.
- Monitor and adjust the hierarchy based on your comfort and progress levels.
- Use positive reinforcement, such as self-reward, after successfully completing desensitization steps.
- Engage in desensitization exercises regularly to build resilience over time.
- Seek guidance from a therapist for adjustments to the desensitization process as needed.
- Share your desensitization goals with a support group for encouragement and accountability.
- Celebrate milestones and achievements throughout the systematic desensitization journey.

Point 3: Tailoring Exposure Techniques to Individual Fears
Overview:
- Explore how exposure techniques can be customized to address specific fears and phobias.

Exploration:
- Understand the diversity of fears and how exposure can be adapted to various contexts.
- Explore case studies or examples where exposure techniques were tailored to specific fears.
- Recognize the importance of personalization in exposure therapy for optimal effectiveness.

- Reflect on your unique fears and consider how exposure might be applied to each.
- Investigate the role of virtual reality or imaginal exposure in addressing specific fears.

Action Steps:
- Identify and prioritize specific fears or phobias you want to target with exposure.
- Research exposure variations suitable for each identified fear or phobia.
- Experiment with different exposure methods to determine the most effective for each fear.
- Gradually expose yourself to fear-inducing situations tailored to each fear category.
- Utilize technology, such as virtual reality apps, if applicable to your exposure goals.
- Join online forums or communities related to specific fears for shared insights and experiences.
- Document your exposure experiences and assess the impact on fear reduction.
- Adjust exposure plans based on feedback from your support system and personal observations.

4: Managing Fear During Exposure

Overview:
- Understand how to effectively manage fear and anxiety during exposure for a successful desensitization process.

Exploration:
- Explore the concept of fear tolerance and its role in exposure therapy.
- Understand the difference between distress and panic during exposure.
- Reflect on past experiences where fear escalated during exposure and analyze contributing factors.
- Explore coping mechanisms commonly used during exposure to manage heightened anxiety.
- Investigate the role of self-talk and cognitive restructuring in reducing fear during exposure.

Action Steps:
- Develop a personalized fear management plan to use during exposure sessions.
- Practice mindfulness techniques to stay present and focused during fear-inducing scenarios.
- Identify and challenge negative thoughts that may escalate fear during exposure.
- Gradually increase exposure intensity while maintaining effective fear management strategies.
- Use relaxation techniques, such as deep breathing, to prevent anxiety from reaching panic levels.
- Integrate positive affirmations into your exposure routine to reinforce a positive mindset.
- Create a "fear toolkit" with items or strategies that provide comfort and reassurance.
- Join support groups or online communities to share and learn from others' fear management experiences.
- Celebrate successful fear management instances as milestones in your exposure journey.

5. Long-Term Maintenance of Exposure Gains

Overview:
- Examine strategies for maintaining the progress achieved through exposure therapy over the long term.

Exploration:
- Explore the concept of relapse prevention in exposure therapy.
- Understand the potential challenges and setbacks that may occur after exposure therapy.
- Reflect on the importance of ongoing, graduated exposure to prevent fear resurgence.
- Examine the role of periodic exposure sessions in maintaining fear reduction gains.
- Consider how lifestyle factors and stress management contribute to maintaining exposure gains.

Action Steps:
- ✓ Integrate mindfulness practices into your daily routine for ongoing emotional balance.
- ✓ Participate in mindfulness workshops or classes to deepen your practice.
- ✓ Explore various mindfulness techniques, such as meditation, mindful breathing, or body scans.
- ✓ Develop awareness of your emotions and their triggers beyond fear.
- ✓ Engage in activities that enhance emotional intelligence, such as journaling or reflective exercises.
- ✓ Seek resources or courses focused on emotional intelligence for continuous improvement.
- ✓ Foster a mindset of continuous learning and personal development.
- ✓ Enroll in courses or workshops that align with your interests and goals.
- ✓ Attend lectures, webinars, or events to expand your knowledge and perspectives.
- ✓ Integrate positive psychology principles into your daily life for sustained well-being.
- ✓ Explore gratitude practices, positive affirmations, and strengths-based activities.
- ✓ Connect with positive psychology communities or forums for ongoing support.
- ✓ Expand your resilience toolkit with additional coping strategies.

- ✓ Experiment with new techniques, such as expressive arts, creative outlets, or physical activities.
- ✓ Collaborate with a mental health professional to customize your toolkit based on evolving needs.
- ✓ Nurture and expand your social support network beyond exposure therapy groups.
- ✓ Engage in social activities, join clubs, or participate in community events.
- ✓ Prioritize authentic connections and contribute positively to your social circles.
- ✓ Investigate holistic approaches to well-being, such as Ayurveda, acupuncture, or energy healing.
- ✓ Consider integrating holistic practices into your routine for comprehensive health benefits.
- ✓ Consult with professionals in holistic well-being for personalized guidance.
- ✓ Maintain a journal documenting your ongoing personal growth and resilience.
- ✓ Reflect on achievements, challenges, and evolving perspectives over time.
- ✓ Share your insights with trusted individuals or contribute to platforms that encourage growth narratives.

Chapter 12

Psychological Approaches:
CBT and Fear Management

1. Cognitive Restructuring: Unraveling Fearful Thoughts
Overview:
- Cognitive Restructuring is a fundamental aspect of CBT, focusing on identifying and challenging negative thought patterns associated with fear.

Exploration:
- Understand the cognitive distortions that contribute to fear, such as catastrophizing or overgeneralization.
- Recognize the impact of irrational thoughts on emotions and behaviors in fear-inducing situations.

Action Steps:
- ✓ Explore cognitive restructuring exercises such as the ABC model (Activating event, Beliefs, Consequences) to identify and challenge negative thought patterns.
- ✓ Develop a habit of immediately countering irrational thoughts with more balanced and objective perspectives.
- ✓ Learn and practice specific CBT tools like cognitive restructuring worksheets that guide you through the process of identifying and reframing negative thoughts.
- ✓ Collaborate with a CBT-trained therapist to tailor these tools to your unique thought patterns and fears.
- ✓ Embrace the Socratic method by consistently asking yourself probing questions to unearth the underlying beliefs and assumptions behind fearful thoughts.
- ✓ Challenge the validity of these assumptions and seek evidence that supports a more rational viewpoint.
- ✓ Integrate mindfulness meditation techniques that specifically focus on observing thoughts without attachment or judgment.
- ✓ Cultivate an attitude of curiosity toward your thoughts, allowing you to distance yourself from automatic, fear-inducing thinking.
- ✓ Develop a set of positive affirmations that counteract common fear-based thoughts.
- ✓ Repeat these affirmations regularly, especially during moments of heightened anxiety, to reinforce positive thinking patterns.

2. Exposure Therapy: Confronting Fear Gradually
Overview:
Exposure therapy involves systematically facing feared stimuli or situations to reduce fear responses over time.

Exploration:
- Identify specific fears and create a hierarchy from least to most anxiety-inducing scenarios.
- Explore the connection between thoughts, emotions, and behaviors during exposure.

Action Steps:
- ✓ Explore the use of virtual reality (VR) exposure therapy under the guidance of mental health professionals.
- ✓ VR can provide realistic simulations of feared situations, enhancing the effectiveness of exposure exercises.
- ✓ Work with a therapist to engage in imaginal exposure, where you vividly imagine feared scenarios in a safe environment.
- ✓ This technique helps desensitize your emotional responses and allows for controlled exploration of feared situations.
- ✓ Cultivate mindfulness techniques to stay present and aware during exposure exercises.
- ✓ Mindfulness can help manage anxiety levels and foster a sense of control over emotional reactions.
- ✓ Collaborate with your therapist to develop graded exposure plans, systematically progressing from less fear-inducing to more challenging scenarios.
- ✓ Break down the exposure hierarchy into manageable steps, ensuring a gradual and structured approach.
- ✓ Leverage online communities or forums where individuals facing similar fears share their exposure experiences.

- ✓ Participate in virtual support groups to exchange insights, encouragement, and advice during the exposure process.
- ✓ Supplement therapist-guided exposure with personalized exposure homework assignments.
- ✓ Gradually increase the difficulty of these assignments based on your comfort level and progress.
- ✓ Consider exposure through various modalities, such as written narratives, drawings, or role-playing.
- ✓ Diversifying exposure methods can enhance the overall effectiveness of desensitization.

3.Cognitive Distortions: Understanding Thought Patterns

Overview:
- • CBT addresses cognitive distortions – biased thought patterns that contribute to fear and anxiety.

Exploration:
- • Identify common cognitive distortions like black-and-white thinking or jumping to conclusions.
- • Examine how these distortions influence perceptions and contribute to fear.

Action Steps:
- ✓ Collaborate with your therapist to design graded exposure plans tailored to the specific fears targeted by cognitive-behavioral therapy (CBT).
- ✓ Graded exposure allows for systematic and controlled confrontation of feared situations.
- ✓ Extend the use of exposure hierarchies to address cognitive challenges associated with fear.
- ✓ Develop a hierarchy that includes thought-triggered anxieties, progressively working from less distressing to more challenging cognitive distortions.
- ✓ Engage in behavioral experiments guided by your therapist to test and challenge irrational thoughts.
- ✓ These experiments provide real-world evidence that can counteract distorted thinking patterns.
- ✓ Integrate mindfulness practices to observe and detach from distorted thoughts without immediate judgment.
- ✓ Mindfulness enhances self-awareness and allows for a more objective examination of cognitive distortions.
- ✓ Collaborate with your therapist to explore and identify core beliefs that contribute to cognitive distortions.
- ✓ Understand how these deep-seated beliefs influence thought patterns and contribute to fear-based thinking.
- ✓ Focus on identifying and challenging catastrophic thinking patterns associated with fear.
- ✓ Work with your therapist to reframe catastrophic thoughts into more balanced and realistic perspectives.
- ✓ Maintain a cognitive journal to document distorted thoughts and their associated emotions.
- ✓ Reflect on patterns and triggers, allowing for a more comprehensive understanding of cognitive distortions.
- ✓ Collaborate with your therapist to develop alternative thought patterns to replace cognitive distortions.

4. Behavioral Techniques: Rewiring Fearful Responses

Overview:
- ✓ Behavioral techniques within CBT aim to modify fear-related behaviors through systematic interventions.

Exploration:
- ✓ Examine how fear influences decision-making and behavioral responses.
- ✓ Understand the role of reinforcement and punishment in perpetuating fear-based behaviors.

Action Steps:
- ✓ Vary the exposure scenarios in behavioral experiments to encompass a range of fear-inducing stimuli.
- ✓ This variability enhances adaptability and reinforces the understanding that fear-related beliefs may not be universally applicable.
- ✓ Maintain a detailed behavioral journal to record responses during exposure exercises.
- ✓ Track not only fear-related behaviors but also any positive or adaptive responses to gradually build a comprehensive understanding.
- ✓ Extend graded exposure beyond structured sessions by incorporating fear-facing scenarios into daily life.
- ✓ This ongoing exposure promotes continuous learning and adaptation to fear-inducing situations.
- ✓ Design a positive reinforcement system that aligns with your personal preferences and motivators.
- ✓ Tailor rewards to adaptive behaviors during fear-facing situations, creating a positive feedback loop.

- ✓ Work closely with your therapist to co-create behavioral intervention plans that align with your specific fears.
- ✓ These plans may include targeted exposure exercises and behavioral strategies tailored to your unique challenges.
- ✓ Explore the use of digital tools or apps to track and analyze behavioral responses systematically.
- ✓ Technology can provide objective data, facilitating a more comprehensive review of progress over time.
- ✓ Consider incorporating virtual reality exposure therapy, guided by a mental health professional.
- ✓ Virtual reality provides a controlled environment for exposure, enhancing the effectiveness of behavioral experiments.
- ✓ Participate in online communities or forums focused on behavioral experiments and exposure therapy.

5. Mindfulness Integration: Fostering Present-Moment Awareness

Overview:
- ✓ Mindfulness practices are integrated into CBT to enhance awareness of thoughts and emotions without immediate judgment.

Exploration:
- ✓ Explore mindfulness techniques, such as breath awareness and body scanning, to cultivate present-moment awareness.
- ✓ Understand how mindfulness contributes to a non-judgmental observation of fear-related thoughts.

Action Steps:
- ✓ Establish daily mindful rituals that serve as anchors for intentional reflection on fear and love.
- ✓ These rituals can include mindful breathing exercises, short meditations, or moments of gratitude.
- ✓ Integrate mindfulness practices directly into exposure exercises, allowing for heightened awareness during fear-facing scenarios.
- ✓ Mindfulness enhances the ability to observe thoughts and emotions without immediate judgment, fostering a more grounded experience.
- ✓ Expand the list of activities that evoke both fear and love to include a diverse range of experiences.
- ✓ Engage in mindfulness during these activities to deepen the connection between present-moment awareness and emotional responses.
- ✓ Form mindfulness partnerships with friends or mentors who share a similar interest in cultivating awareness.
- ✓ Regularly discuss and exchange insights from your mindfulness practices, creating a supportive environment for personal growth.
- ✓ Enrich your mindfulness journey by actively participating in workshops, courses, or local communities dedicated to mindfulness.
- ✓ Engage with like-minded individuals, share experiences, and learn from diverse perspectives on incorporating mindfulness into daily life.
- ✓ Create visual or auditory reminders throughout the day to prompt moments of intentional reflection.
- ✓ These reminders can be subtle cues, such as a notification on your phone or a symbol in your environment, signaling the need for mindfulness.

Chapter 13

Mindfulness and Meditation:
Calming the Fearful Mind

1.Mindfulness Foundations: Building a Grounded Practice
Overview:
- Mindfulness is the practice of cultivating present-moment awareness without judgment. Establishing a solid foundation is crucial for calming the fearful mind.

Exploration:
- Reflect on the core principles of mindfulness: attention to the present, acceptance of thoughts and feelings, and non-reactivity.
- Explore different mindfulness meditation techniques, such as focused attention, body scan, and loving-kindness meditation.

Action Steps:
- Clear the designated space of unnecessary items to minimize distractions.
- Consider incorporating calming elements, such as soft lighting or soothing colors.
- Personalize the space with items that evoke a sense of peace, creating a mindful atmosphere.
- Initiate with 5-10 minute sessions and add a few minutes as comfort and concentration grow.
- Pay attention to the quality of your practice, prioritizing mindful presence over session length.
- Celebrate small milestones, reinforcing positive associations with extended practice.
- Incorporate guided sessions led by experienced meditation teachers or through reputable apps.
- Experiment with different themes, such as body scans, loving-kindness, or breath-focused meditations.
- Gradually transition to unguided sessions as your confidence and comfort with silent meditation increase.
- Begin each session with a few minutes of intentional focus on the breath.
- Notice the sensations of inhalation and exhalation, fostering a heightened awareness of the present.
- Use the breath as a grounding tool throughout the day during moments of stress or distraction.
- Set specific times for mindfulness practice, aligning them with periods of the day conducive to focus.
- Integrate mindfulness into existing routines, such as morning rituals or pre-sleep practices.
- Communicate your commitment to mindfulness to those around you, minimizing potential interruptions.

2. Mindful Body Scan: Cultivating Awareness from Within
Overview:
- Body scan meditation involves systematically directing attention through different parts of the body, promoting deep relaxation and heightened self-awareness.

Exploration:
- Reflect on the mind-body connection and how bodily sensations relate to emotional states.
- Consider the impact of stress and tension on the body, recognizing areas where fear manifests physically.

Action Steps:
- Choose a reputable guided body scan meditation, led by an experienced instructor or through meditation apps.
- Start each session by lying down or sitting comfortably, progressively directing attention from the head to the toes.
- Observe changes in body awareness and mental states after incorporating guided body scans into your routine.
- Practice acknowledging bodily sensations without attaching labels of 'good' or 'bad.'
- Cultivate an open and curious mindset, exploring sensations with gentle attention.
- Apply non-judgmental awareness to daily activities, extending the practice beyond formal meditation sessions.
- Set reminders to conduct brief body scans during breaks at work or routine activities.

- Direct attention to different body regions, even for a few minutes, fostering continual mindfulness.
- Notice any shifts in mental focus and stress levels by incorporating intermittent body scans into your daily rhythm.
- Coordinate your breath with the progression of attention during a body scan, syncing inhalation and exhalation with different body regions.
- Experiment with variations, such as inhaling energy into specific areas and exhaling tension or discomfort.
- Incorporate coordinated breath and body awareness during meditation and extend it to mindful moments throughout the day.
- Explore mindful walking by paying attention to the sensations in your feet, legs, and body as you move.
- Integrate sitting body scans into meditation sessions, adapting the practice to different postures.
- Notice which variations resonate most with you, and customize your routine accordingly for a well-rounded mindfulness experience.

3. Loving-Kindness Meditation: Fostering Compassion Amid Fear
Overview:
- Loving-kindness meditation, or "Metta," involves sending well-wishes to oneself and others, fostering compassion and reducing fear.

Exploration:
- Reflect on the interconnectedness of emotions and how cultivating love and compassion can counteract fear.
- Consider the role of self-compassion in mitigating fear-driven thoughts and behaviors.

Action Steps:
- Set aside dedicated time each day for a loving-kindness meditation focused on self-compassion.
- Begin with acknowledging your inherent worth and extending well-wishes to yourself.
- Observe changes in your self-perception and emotional resilience over time.
- In your meditation, progressively include specific individuals within your inner circle.
- Cultivate a sense of warmth and love towards these individuals, fostering stronger emotional connections.
- Notice shifts in your relationships and your own emotional responses as you expand your circle.
- Incorporate people you encounter regularly but may not have close ties with into your meditation practice.
- Cultivate a genuine sense of care and well-wishing for their happiness and peace.
- Observe any changes in your perceptions of these individuals and your interactions with them.

4.Mindfulness in Daily Activities: Infusing the Ordinary with Presence
Overview:
- Extend mindfulness beyond formal meditation by incorporating it into daily activities, transforming routine tasks into opportunities for presence.

Exploration:
- Reflect on the habitual nature of daily tasks and how mindfulness can shift these experiences.
- Consider how fear influences the quality of your engagement in routine activities.

Action Steps:
- Choose activities like dishwashing, showering, or commuting to practice mindful appreciation.
- Engage your senses fully, noticing textures, smells, and sounds during these activities.
- Observe any shifts in your mindset and appreciation for the present moment.
- Set periodic alarms or notifications to remind you to take a few mindful breaths.
- Use these moments to pause, close your eyes, and focus on the sensation of your breath.
- Notice any changes in your stress levels, mood, or overall mental clarity.
- Prioritize active listening in conversations, allowing others to express themselves fully.
- Avoid formulating responses in your mind while the other person is speaking.
- Notice any improvements in the quality of your relationships and communication.
- During walks or outdoor activities, focus on the sights, sounds, and sensations of nature.
- Practice mindful breathing in natural settings, fostering a connection with the environment.
- Observe any changes in your mood, stress levels, or sense of connection with nature.

- Schedule short breaks throughout the day for mindfulness exercises.
- Choose activities like mindful breathing, stretching, or a brief meditation during breaks.
- Monitor changes in your focus, energy levels, and overall work engagement.

5. Mindfulness for Emotional Regulation: Navigating Fearful Emotions

Overview:
- Mindfulness can be a powerful tool for regulating emotions, allowing a more balanced response to fearful thoughts and feelings.

Exploration:
- Reflect on the role of mindfulness in observing emotions without becoming overwhelmed by them.
- Explore how fear affects emotional regulation and how mindfulness can provide a buffer.

Action Steps:
- Journal about fear-triggering situations, describing emotions with mindfulness and without judgment.
- Explore patterns in emotional responses, fostering a deeper understanding of fear triggers.
- Practice body scan meditations during moments of fear, observing sensations from head to toe.
- Notice how physical reactions align with emotional responses, promoting mind-body connection.
- When faced with fear, take a deliberate pause before responding, focusing on the breath.
- Consider how these pauses influence the overall dynamics of fear-inducing situations.
- Set alarms or reminders for brief mindfulness check-ins, observing thoughts and emotions.
- Use these moments during fear-inducing situations to cultivate present-moment awareness.
- Research and enroll in reputable MBSR programs available online or in your community.
- Commit to the program, engaging in various mindfulness practices and reflections.

The Power of Breathwork in Quieting Fear

1. The Basics of Breathwork for Fear Reduction:

Overview:
- Breathwork is an ancient practice rooted in various cultures and traditions worldwide, acknowledging the profound connection between breath, mind, and body.
- Recognizing breath as a powerful and accessible tool for managing and alleviating fear.

Exploration:
- Delve into how intentional breathing influences the autonomic nervous system, transitioning the body from a state of heightened arousal (sympathetic) to a more relaxed state (parasympathetic).
- Contemplate the impact of breath on physiological responses such as heart rate, blood pressure, and the release of stress-related hormones.
- Explore the psychological benefits of intentional breathing in fostering mental clarity, focus, and emotional regulation during moments of fear.
- Reflect on the interplay between breath and the mind, recognizing the potential to calm and center the mental state.

Action Steps:
- Begin the breathwork journey with simple breath awareness exercises, allowing yourself to observe the natural rhythm without attempting to alter or control it.
- Cultivate a non-judgmental awareness of the breath, focusing on its flow without immediate interference.
- Start by dedicating short periods, perhaps a few minutes, to mindful breathing, allowing for a gentle initiation into the practice.
- Gradually extend the duration of these mindful breathing sessions as comfort and familiarity with the practice grow.
- Progress from simple breath awareness to diaphragmatic breathing, emphasizing deep inhalations that expand the diaphragm and slow, deliberate exhalations.
- Understand the role of the diaphragm in this technique, promoting a more profound and controlled breath cycle.
- Experiment with diaphragmatic breathing in various postures, such as seated or lying down, to find the most comfortable and effective approach.
- Explore how different postures influence the depth and ease of diaphragmatic breathing, tailoring the practice to suit individual preferences.
- Notice any correlations between your breath and emotional states, laying the foundation for future emotional regulation.

2. The Mind-Body Connection through Breath:
Overview:
- Begin by recognizing the profound and intricate link between breath and the mind, acknowledging that the way we breathe directly affects our mental and emotional states.
- Understand that the breath serves as a bridge connecting the physiological and psychological aspects of our being, influencing our response to fear.

Exploration:
- Reflect on personal experiences or instances where conscious, intentional breathing has led to a noticeable calming effect on heightened states of fear or anxiety.
- Consider the transformative power of breath in modulating emotional responses and perceptions of fear, fostering a sense of control and centeredness.

Action Steps:
- Actively practice mindful breathing during fear-inducing situations, recognizing the breath as a grounding force.
- Consciously bring attention to the breath, allowing it to serve as a focal point amidst heightened emotions.
- Observe how conscious breathing functions as a buffer between the initial surge of fear and subsequent emotional and cognitive responses.
- Recognize the breath's role in creating a momentary pause, providing space for a more intentional and measured reaction to fear.
- Expand your breathwork repertoire by exploring techniques such as box breathing (equal duration of inhalation, hold, exhalation) or the 4-7-8 technique (inhale for 4 counts, hold for 7, exhale for 8).
- Experimentation with different techniques allows for the identification of variations that resonate most effectively in different fear contexts.

3. Breathwork Techniques for Different Fear Scenarios:
Overview:
- Acknowledge the versatility of breathwork as a tool adaptable to a range of fears and anxieties, emphasizing the importance of tailoring techniques to specific scenarios.
- Understand that a nuanced approach to breathwork allows for a more precise and effective response to diverse fear manifestations.

Exploration:
- Identify and categorize different fear scenarios, recognizing that fears can vary in intensity, triggers, and emotional responses.
- Understand the unique qualities of each fear scenario, such as acute panic, anticipatory anxiety, or generalized unease.

Action Steps:
- Actively engage in the exploration and practice of a diverse range of breathwork techniques, including diaphragmatic breathing, box breathing, rhythmic breathing, and more.
- Embrace the opportunity to experience the unique qualities and effects of each technique.
- Tailor your selection of breathwork techniques based on the specific characteristics of different fear scenarios.
- Consider the nature and intensity of the fear, adapting your approach to suit the context and your personal comfort.
- Systematically organize a personalized "breath toolkit" that includes a diverse set of breathwork practices.
- Categorize techniques based on their purposes, such as calming, grounding, or energizing, allowing for easy navigation and selection.
- Classify each breathwork technique according to its suitability for different intensities and manifestations of fear.
- Recognize that certain techniques may be more effective in acute moments of fear, while others may be beneficial for ongoing stress management.
- Ensure that your "breath toolkit" is easily accessible, either physically or through digital means, allowing for quick and intuitive access in the moment.

4. Integrating Breathwork into Daily Life:
Overview:
- Recognize breathwork as a transformative tool with the potential to enhance overall well-being when seamlessly woven into daily life.
- Understand that the cumulative effects of consistent breathwork extend beyond individual moments, contributing to a heightened sense of fear resilience.

Exploration:
- Reflect on the sustained impact of consistent breathwork practices on emotional, mental, and physical aspects of fear resilience.
- Consider how regular integration contributes to an ongoing state of balance, reducing the likelihood of fear escalation.

Action Steps:
- Integrate short breathwork sessions into your morning and evening routines to establish positive intentions and promote relaxation.
- Begin your day with intentional breathing to set a mindful tone, and conclude it with breathwork to unwind and release tension.
- Designate specific times for focused breathwork, aligning with the natural rhythm of waking up and winding down.
- Choose moments that complement your circadian rhythms, such as awakening and before bedtime, for enhanced effectiveness.
- Use breathwork as a transition tool between different activities, providing a brief pause for intentional and centered breathing.
- Before moving from one task to another, engage in a few minutes of focused breathwork to create a seamless and mindful shift.
- Cultivate awareness during transitions between activities, allowing breathwork to serve as a bridge between moments of stress and calm.
- As you move from work to a break or from a busy environment to a quieter one, use breathwork to consciously shift your mental state.

5. Advanced Breathwork Practices for Fear Mastery:
Overview:
- Delve into advanced breathwork practices as a means to attain a profound mastery of the fear response.
- Recognize that advanced techniques offer nuanced approaches to cultivating resilience and heightened self-awareness.

Exploration:
- Reflect on personal experiences with advanced breathwork techniques and their impact on the perception and management of fear.
- Consider how these practices have influenced not only immediate fear responses but also long-term emotional resilience.

Action Steps:
- Begin by experimenting with longer breath retention periods during breathwork sessions, progressively extending the duration as comfort allows.
- Gradually increase the time of breath retention, paying attention to your body's signals and ensuring a gradual and comfortable progression.
- Embrace the challenge of extended breath retention, acknowledging its potential to deepen the mind-body connection and enhance emotional regulation.
- Understand that prolonged breath retention can be a powerful tool for cultivating heightened awareness and resilience.
- Explore guided breathwork sessions or workshops facilitated by experienced practitioners to gain in-depth knowledge and guidance.
- Seek out workshops that focus on advanced techniques, ensuring that the facilitator has expertise in guiding participants through more intricate breathwork practices.
- Attend sessions that specialize in advanced breathwork techniques, providing a structured environment for exploration and learning.
- Look for workshops or classes that specifically target mastery of breathwork and offer a supportive community for those seeking to deepen their practice.

The Role of Diet and Exercise in Reducing Anxiety

1. The Impact of Nutrition on Anxiety:

Overview:
- Understand that nutrition plays a crucial role in mental health, including anxiety.
- Recognize the connection between dietary choices, neurotransmitter production, and overall emotional well-being.
- Acknowledge the potential of certain nutrients to either exacerbate or alleviate anxiety symptoms.

Exploration:
- Reflect on personal dietary habits and their potential influence on anxiety levels.
- Explore scientific literature and studies on the relationship between specific nutrients, such as omega-3 fatty acids and magnesium, and anxiety reduction.
- Consider consulting with a nutritionist or healthcare professional to assess dietary patterns and identify areas for improvement.

Action Steps:
- Gradually transition to a diet that includes a variety of fruits, vegetables, whole grains, lean proteins, and healthy fats.
- Experiment with different recipes and cooking methods to make meals both nutritious and enjoyable.
- Keep a food diary to track dietary changes and assess their impact on mood and anxiety levels.
- Set realistic and achievable goals for dietary improvements, ensuring a sustainable approach to long-term health.
- Include fatty fish, such as salmon or trout, in your diet at least twice a week to benefit from omega-3 fatty acids.
- Snack on a handful of nuts or seeds, like walnuts or sunflower seeds, to introduce anxiety-reducing nutrients into your daily routine.
- Experiment with diverse leafy greens in salads or smoothies to increase magnesium intake.
- Explore recipes that incorporate berries, such as blueberries or strawberries, as a delicious and nutritious addition to meals.

2. Exercise as a Natural Anxiety Regulator:

Overview:
- Recognize the role of physical activity in regulating neurotransmitters and reducing stress hormones.
- Understand that consistent exercise is associated with improved mood and decreased anxiety.
- Acknowledge the diverse forms of exercise and their potential benefits for individuals with varying preferences.

Exploration:
- Reflect on personal experiences with exercise and its impact on mood and anxiety levels.
- Explore different types of physical activities, including aerobic exercises, strength training, and mind-body practices like yoga.
- Investigate the connection between exercise frequency, intensity, and duration in relation to anxiety reduction.

Action Steps:
- Set realistic and achievable exercise goals, considering individual fitness levels and preferences.
- Schedule dedicated time for exercise in the weekly routine, treating it as a non-negotiable aspect of self-care.
- Experiment with various forms of exercise, such as walking, jogging, cycling, or swimming, to find activities that resonate with personal interests.
- Choose activities that bring a sense of pleasure and satisfaction, whether it's dancing, hiking, or playing a sport.
- Experiment with different exercise classes or group activities to discover new and engaging ways to stay active.
- Involve friends or family in exercise routines, transforming physical activity into a social and enjoyable experience.
- Begin with low to moderate-intensity exercises, such as brisk walking or gentle yoga, especially for beginners.
- Gradually incorporate more challenging activities, such as jogging or resistance training, as fitness levels improve.

- Listen to the body and adjust exercise intensity based on individual comfort and progression.

3. The Gut-Brain Connection:

Overview:
- Understand the bidirectional relationship between the gut and the brain, known as the gut-brain axis.
- Recognize the influence of gut health on mental well-being, including anxiety levels.
- Acknowledge the role of a balanced microbiome in supporting emotional resilience.

Exploration:
- Reflect on dietary habits and their potential impact on gut health.
- Explore the concept of gut dysbiosis and its association with mental health conditions, including anxiety.
- Consider the use of probiotics and prebiotics as interventions to support a healthy gut.

Action Steps:
- Gradually incorporate more fruits and vegetables into daily meals, aiming for a colorful and diverse plate.
- Experiment with whole grains such as quinoa, brown rice, and oats as alternatives to refined grains.
- Include legumes like beans and lentils in soups, salads, or main dishes to boost fiber content.
- Include a serving of fermented foods in daily meals, such as yogurt with live cultures or a side of sauerkraut.
- Experiment with homemade fermented options to customize flavors and incorporate diverse strains of probiotics.
- Monitor how the introduction of fermented foods impacts digestion and overall well-being.
- Schedule a consultation with a healthcare professional or nutritionist to discuss specific gut health goals.
- Share relevant information about dietary habits, lifestyle, and any digestive symptoms experienced.
- Implement recommendations provided by professionals, incorporating them gradually into daily routines.

4. Holistic Lifestyle Modifications:

Overview:
- Recognize that anxiety reduction involves a holistic approach, incorporating various lifestyle factors.
- Understand the interconnectedness of sleep, stress management, and social connections with anxiety levels.
- Acknowledge the potential compounding effects of unhealthy lifestyle choices on anxiety.

Exploration:
- Reflect on the quality and duration of sleep, recognizing its impact on anxiety.
- Explore stress management techniques such as meditation, deep breathing, or mindfulness practices.
- Consider the role of social support and meaningful connections in promoting emotional well-being.

Action Steps:
- Establish a regular sleep routine by going to bed and waking up at the same time each day.
- Create a comfortable sleep environment, minimizing disturbances such as noise and light.
- Practice relaxation techniques, such as deep breathing or gentle stretches, before bedtime.
- Dedicate time daily to stress-reduction activities, such as guided meditation or deep relaxation exercises.
- Experiment with various techniques to find the most effective ones for alleviating stress.
- Consider integrating mindfulness into routine activities, fostering a continuous sense of calm.
- Schedule regular social activities with friends, family, or supportive individuals.
- Communicate openly with trusted individuals about feelings and experiences related to anxiety.
- Join social groups or communities that align with personal interests, expanding the social support network.

5. Professional Guidance and Monitoring:

Overview:
- Recognize the importance of seeking professional guidance for personalized anxiety management.
- Understand that healthcare professionals, including nutritionists, therapists, and fitness experts, can provide tailored recommendations.
- Acknowledge the need for ongoing monitoring and adjustments to lifestyle modifications.

Exploration:

- Explore available mental health resources, including therapists, counselors, and registered dietitians.
- Research evidence-based interventions and modalities for anxiety reduction, considering individual preferences and needs.
- Understand the potential benefits of multidisciplinary approaches involving professionals from different fields.

Action Steps:

- Schedule an appointment with a healthcare professional, such as a primary care physician, to discuss anxiety concerns.
- Collaborate with the healthcare professional to create a personalized plan addressing dietary, exercise, and lifestyle factors.
- Discuss any potential medical considerations that may impact anxiety and explore appropriate interventions.
- Schedule sessions with a mental health professional, such as a therapist or counselor, to discuss anxiety management.
- Collaborate on developing coping strategies that align with personal preferences and lifestyle.
- Explore therapeutic interventions, such as cognitive-behavioral therapy (CBT) or mindfulness-based approaches, based on professional recommendations.
- Establish a routine for self-monitoring, incorporating reflections on dietary choices, exercise habits, and stress levels.
- Regularly reassess lifestyle modifications, considering both positive outcomes and areas for improvement.
- Be open to making adjustments to the anxiety management plan based on evolving needs and feedback from healthcare and mental health professionals.
- Schedule a consultation with a registered dietitian to discuss dietary habits and their impact on anxiety.
- Collaborate on creating a nutritional plan that aligns with individual preferences and dietary requirements.
- Seek ongoing support and guidance from the registered dietitian to ensure the successful implementation of dietary changes.

Chapter 14

Building Resilience:
The Pillar of Fearless Living

1. Building Resilience: The Pillar of Fearless Living
Overview:
- Resilience stands as the bedrock of fearless living, constituting the fortitude that enables individuals to confront and overcome life's myriad challenges, fostering strength, adaptability, and personal growth.
- At its essence, resilience is not a fixed trait but a dynamic and malleable quality that individuals can cultivate and enhance over time.
- It serves as a shield against the adversities one may encounter, allowing for a proactive response to stressors and setbacks.

Exploration:
- Delve into the multi-faceted nature of resilience, recognizing it as a process that encompasses psychological, emotional, and social dimensions.
- Explore how resilience manifests in various aspects of life, influencing the ability to bounce back from setbacks, maintain emotional equilibrium, and sustain a positive outlook even in challenging circumstances.
- Understand resilience as a skill set that can be developed, refined, and applied across different life domains.

Action Steps:
- ✓ Embrace challenges as opportunities for personal development.
- ✓ Foster a belief in continuous learning and adaptation.
- ✓ Cultivate meaningful relationships that provide emotional support.
- ✓ Share experiences and challenges with trusted friends or mentors.
- ✓ Develop a kind and understanding attitude toward yourself, especially during setbacks.
- ✓ Reframe negative self-talk into positive and affirming statements.
- ✓ Break down larger objectives into manageable, achievable tasks.
- ✓ Celebrate small victories and progress to reinforce resilience.
- ✓ Establish consistent self-care routines that address physical, emotional, and mental well-being.
- ✓ Ensure sufficient rest, nutrition, and moments of relaxation.

2. Enhancing Emotional Intelligence: Navigating Feelings with Finesse
Overview:
- Emotional intelligence emerges as a pivotal element in the tapestry of fearless living, providing individuals with the acumen to comprehend, regulate, and harness emotions adeptly. This skill set not only fosters profound self-awareness but also empowers individuals to navigate the complex terrain of interpersonal relationships with finesse.

Exploration:
- Dive into the realm of self-awareness, understanding one's emotions, strengths, weaknesses, and the impact emotions have on thoughts and behaviors.
- Explore the capacity for self-regulation, which involves managing and redirecting disruptive emotions to maintain composure and make sound decisions.
- Delve into the ability to empathize, comprehending others' emotions and perspectives, fostering deeper connections and understanding in relationships.
- Understand the motivational aspect of emotional intelligence, where individuals can harness emotions to drive them toward achieving goals and sustaining resilience.
- Explore the domain of social skills, encompassing effective communication, conflict resolution, and the ability to build and nurture meaningful relationships.
- Unpack the symbiotic relationship between emotional intelligence and resilience, recognizing how a heightened understanding of emotions equips individuals to adapt to challenges with greater ease.

- Explore how emotional intelligence acts as a guiding compass in decision-making, enabling individuals to make choices that align with their values and contribute to a fearless, purpose-driven life.

Action Steps:
- Regularly engage in self-reflection to understand personal emotions and triggers.
- Identify patterns of emotional responses in various situations.
- Develop mindfulness practices to observe and regulate emotional reactions.
- Utilize techniques like deep breathing or brief pauses in challenging situations.
- Practice active listening to understand others' perspectives.
- Cultivate empathy by acknowledging and validating the feelings of those around you.
- Align personal goals with intrinsic motivations for sustained enthusiasm.
- Break down larger goals into smaller, achievable steps for continuous motivation.
- Strengthen communication skills, fostering positive interactions.
- Engage in group activities or collaborative projects to enhance social skills.

3. The Art of Decision-Making: Empowering Choices for Fearless Living
Overview:
- The art of decision-making stands tall as a fundamental pillar in the architecture of fearless living, wielding profound influence over the paths we tread and the destinations we reach.
- Empowering choices are not merely a consequence but a deliberate, skillful craft that shapes the narrative of one's life.

Exploration:
- Delve into the rational decision-making model, where individuals systematically analyze options, weigh pros and cons, and make choices aligned with logical considerations.
- Explore the intuitive side of decision-making, acknowledging the role of gut feelings, instincts, and implicit knowledge in steering choices.
- Understand decision-making through the lens of behavioral economics, examining how psychological factors and biases influence economic decisions.
- Unpack the impact of confirmation bias, where individuals tend to favor information that confirms preexisting beliefs, shaping decisions in a way that aligns with their worldview.
- Explore how anchoring bias influences decisions by relying heavily on the first piece of information encountered, anchoring subsequent judgments.
- Understand the role of loss aversion, where the fear of loss often leads individuals to make choices that minimize potential losses rather than maximizing gains.
- Investigate the symbiotic relationship between effective decision-making and confidence, recognizing how making informed choices enhances self-assurance.
- Explore how the decision-making process contributes to resilience, emphasizing the capacity to adapt and bounce back regardless of the outcomes.

Action Steps:
- ✓ Identify and prioritize personal values to guide decision-making. - Evaluate choices based on alignment with these core values.
- ✓ Embrace calculated risks as opportunities for growth.
- ✓ Balance risk-taking with a realistic assessment of potential outcomes.
- ✓ Apply mindfulness to decision-making, staying present and focused.
- ✓ Avoid overthinking by making choices based on the current situation and available information.
- ✓ View mistakes as learning opportunities, promoting a growth mindset.
- ✓ Reflect on past decisions to refine future choices.
- ✓ Gather input from diverse sources to make well-informed decisions.
- ✓ Consider alternative viewpoints to broaden understanding.

4. Cultivating Positive Habits: Sustaining Resilience in Daily Practices
Overview:
- ✓ Positive habits contribute significantly to building resilience and fostering a fearless mindset, shaping a foundation for consistent well-being.

Exploration:
- Explore the science of habit formation and its impact on brain plasticity.
- Understand the link between positive habits, self-discipline, and long-term resilience.

Action Steps:
- Begin with small, manageable habits to establish a foundation. - Gradually expand positive habits to encompass a broader spectrum of well-being.
- Integrate new habits with existing daily routines for seamless adoption.
- Utilize triggers from existing activities to cue the initiation of new habits.
- Prioritize consistency in habit formation over intensity.
- Build habits incrementally, ensuring they align with personal values.
- Maintain a habit journal to track progress and identify challenges.
- Celebrate small victories to reinforce positive behavior.
- Share habit goals with a friend or family member for mutual accountability.
- Join communities or forums focused on habit-building for added support.

5. Building Social Resilience: Nurturing Connections for Fearless Living
Overview:
- Social connections are integral to resilience, providing support and a sense of belonging crucial for fearless living.

Exploration:
- Explore the impact of social relationships on mental health and resilience.
- Understand the dynamics of healthy interpersonal connections.

Action Steps:
- Invest time in building deep, meaningful connections. - Prioritize quality over quantity in social relationships.
- Develop active listening skills to enhance communication.
- Express thoughts and feelings openly, fostering understanding.
- Learn constructive conflict resolution techniques for healthier relationships.
- Address conflicts promptly and with empathy.
- Establish clear personal boundaries in relationships.
- Communicate and reinforce boundaries for mutual respect.
- Engage in community activities or volunteering for a sense of purpose.
- Build a supportive network within communities of shared interests.

Chapter 15

The Courage to Fail:
Embracing Mistakes Without Fear

1. The Courage to Fail: Embracing Mistakes Without Fear
Overview:
- Recognizing and embracing failure is fundamental to fearless living, challenging societal norms and fostering an environment where mistakes are seen as opportunities for growth.

Exploration:
- Recognize the transformative potential of reframing failure as a catalyst for personal and professional development.
- Explore how embracing failure enhances resilience, enabling individuals to navigate challenges with increased strength.
- Understand that mistakes offer valuable learning opportunities, contributing to innovation and self-discovery.
- Delve into the psychological dimensions of the fear of failure, examining its impact on decision-making and risk-taking.
- Develop strategies for building resilience against shame, separating one's self-worth from mistakes.

Action Steps:
- Recognize instances of a fixed mindset, where failure is viewed as a reflection of personal abilities, and actively work towards adopting a growth mindset.
- Incorporate positive affirmations that emphasize the potential for growth and development inherent in every failure.
- Reflect on past failures, extracting lessons learned and acknowledging personal growth resulting from those experiences.
- Develop a personalized toolkit comprising coping mechanisms, support networks, and self-compassion strategies to navigate failure.
- Cultivate a mindset of celebration for small failures, recognizing them as indicators of stepping out of comfort zones.

2. The Courage to Fail: Embracing Mistakes Without Fear
Overview:
- Recognizing and embracing failure is fundamental to fearless living, challenging societal norms and fostering an environment where mistakes are seen as opportunities for growth.

Exploration:
- Recognize the transformative potential of reframing failure as a catalyst for personal and professional development.
- Explore how embracing failure enhances resilience, enabling individuals to navigate challenges with increased strength.
- Understand that mistakes offer valuable learning opportunities, contributing to innovation and self-discovery.
- Delve into the psychological dimensions of the fear of failure, examining its impact on decision-making and risk-taking.
- Develop strategies for building resilience against shame, separating one's self-worth from mistakes.

Action Steps:
- Recognize instances of a fixed mindset, where failure is viewed as a reflection of personal abilities, and actively work towards adopting a growth mindset.
- ***Positive Affirmations:*** Incorporate positive affirmations that emphasize the potential for growth and development inherent in every failure.
- Engage in fear-setting exercises to pinpoint specific fears associated with failure, dissecting them to diminish their impact.
- Deliberate on worst-case scenarios, realizing that often imagined consequences are exaggerated, leading to greater fear than necessary.

- Reflect on past failures, extracting lessons learned and acknowledging personal growth resulting from those experiences.

3. Nurturing Authentic Connections: Building a Fearless Social Network

Overview:
- Fearless living thrives in the presence of authentic connections, emphasizing the quality and depth of relationships over mere quantity.

Exploration:
- Explore the impact of deep, meaningful connections on emotional well-being and resilience.
- *Vulnerability and Trust:* Examine the role of vulnerability and trust in fostering authentic connections, creating spaces for open communication.
- Investigate the importance of expressing one's true self within relationships, fostering an environment where authenticity is valued.
- Explore the discomfort that may accompany authentic interactions, acknowledging it as a necessary part of genuine connections.
- Evaluate the impact of digital communication on the depth of connections, seeking a balance between online and offline interactions.
- Examine the fear of missing out (FOMO) in the context of social connections, cultivating contentment with the quality of relationships.

Action Steps:
- Foster open communication by sharing thoughts, feelings, and experiences authentically.
- Encourage the acceptance of imperfections in oneself and others, creating an atmosphere of authenticity.
- Prioritize quality time in existing relationships, engaging in meaningful activities that strengthen connections.

4. Unleashing Creativity: Expressing Fearlessness Through Artistic Endeavors

Overview:
- Fearless living finds expression in the boundless realms of creativity, encouraging individuals to explore and express themselves through artistic mediums.

Exploration:
- Delve into various artistic mediums as tools for self-discovery, providing avenues for exploring emotions and perspectives.
- Understand how creative expression serves as a mirror, reflecting aspects of oneself that may not be immediately apparent.
- Address the fear of judgment and creative inhibition, creating environments that encourage experimentation and risk-taking.
- Shift the focus from the final product to the creative process, fostering a fearless attitude toward exploration.

Action Steps:
- Dedicate time to explore a variety of artistic mediums, identifying those that resonate most personally.
- Adopt a mindset of continuous experimentation, embracing new artistic endeavors without the pressure of mastery.
- Establish a judgment-free space for artistic expression, emphasizing the value of the creative process over the end result.
- Participate in or initiate community art projects, fostering a sense of collective creativity.
- Engage in collaborative artistic projects, tapping into the synergy of shared creativity.
- *Cross-Disciplinary Exploration:* Explore connections between different artistic disciplines, expanding creative boundaries.
- Incorporate brief, daily artistic practices into routines, cultivating a consistent and sustainable creative outlet.

5. Physical Mastery: Cultivating Fearlessness Through Movement

Overview:
- Physical mastery is a cornerstone of fearless living, promoting a harmonious relationship between the body and mind through intentional movement.

Exploration:

- Explore the concept of embodied presence, acknowledging the profound connection between physical movement and mental well-being.
- Understand the role of somatic awareness in cultivating a mindful and fearless approach to movement.
- Examine how physical exercise empowers individuals, fostering a sense of strength and capability.
- Integrate mindfulness into movement practices, elevating the experience beyond mere physical activity.
- Encourage stepping beyond physical comfort zones, whether through new sports, dance forms, or outdoor activities.
- Embrace the spirit of play in physical activities, viewing them as opportunities for joyful exploration.

Action Steps:
- Conduct a personal movement assessment, identifying preferred and unexplored forms of physical activity.
- Establish goals for physical exploration, prioritizing activities that align with personal interests and passions.
- Incorporate mindful warm-ups into exercise routines, connecting with the body before engaging in more intense physical activity.
- Cultivate a body-positive mindset by incorporating affirmations during exercise, focusing on strength and vitality.
- Participate in group fitness classes, leveraging the collective energy and support of a community.
- Engage in team sports to foster cooperation, communication, and a shared sense of accomplishment.
- Integrate outdoor activities and nature exploration into physical routines, harnessing the rejuvenating power of the natural environment.
- Balance solo outdoor adventures with group activities, enjoying both self-reflection and shared experiences.
- Explore holistic practices like yoga, tai chi, or mindful dance, emphasizing the integration of mind and body.
- Schedule regular physical assessments to track progress, celebrate achievements, and adapt routines accordingly.

Chapter 16

Storytelling and Fear:
Rewriting Your Narrative

1. Transformative Power of Personal Narratives:
Overviews:
- Personal narratives wield a profound influence on how individuals perceive and believe in the face of fear, acting as powerful lenses that color our worldview.
- Understanding the transformative potency of storytelling provides individuals with the means to reclaim agency over their narratives, steering them away from disempowering narratives.
- Storytelling becomes a catalyst for a paradigm shift, enabling individuals to transcend a victimhood mentality and embrace empowerment, fostering resilience in the face of fear.
- Exploring personal narratives serves as a revealing journey, uncovering recurrent patterns and themes that contribute to the manifestation of fear, offering insights for transformative change.
- Embracing storytelling as a dynamic tool for change empowers individuals to rewrite their narratives actively, fostering a resilient mindset that can navigate and conquer fears.

Explorations:
- Take the time to reflect on significant moments in your life, identifying the narratives intertwined with fear and acknowledging their impact on your perception.
- Explore how personal narratives shape your self-perception, influencing how you view your capabilities, strengths, and vulnerabilities in the face of challenges.
- Examine the broader context by delving into the role of storytelling in cultural and societal settings, recognizing how collective narratives impact shared fears.
- Investigate narratives propagated by various media sources and their role in shaping public perception of fear, considering the influence on societal attitudes.
- Understand the underlying psychological mechanisms by which narratives mold our understanding of fear, delving into cognitive processes and emotional responses.

Action Steps:
- Initiate a personal storytelling practice, documenting experiences related to fear.
- Engage in narrative therapy or counseling to explore and reshape your relationship with fear.
- Collaborate with a mentor or support group to share and reshape narratives collectively.
- Experiment with creative expressions such as writing, art, or performance to tell your story.
- Develop a habit of reframing negative narratives into empowering ones, focusing on growth.

2. The Role of Cultural Narratives in Fear Perception:
Overviews:
- Cultural narratives significantly influence how individuals perceive and respond to fear.
- Understanding cultural stories allows for a nuanced exploration of shared fears and coping mechanisms.
- Cultural narratives can either amplify or mitigate individual fears, depending on societal values.
- Recognizing the impact of cultural storytelling on collective fears is crucial for fostering empathy.
- Empowering cultural narratives can contribute to a more resilient and fearless society.

Explorations:
- Analyze cultural stories, myths, and legends that shape perceptions of fear in your community.
- Explore how cultural narratives evolve and adapt to address contemporary fears.
- Investigate the role of storytelling in cultural rituals and practices related to fear.
- Examine how diverse cultural narratives contribute to a broader understanding of fear.
- Reflect on personal beliefs influenced by cultural narratives and their impact on your fears.

Action Steps:
- Engage in cross-cultural dialogues to broaden your perspective on storytelling and fear.
- Participate in or initiate community storytelling events to share diverse narratives.
- Support initiatives that amplify positive and empowering cultural narratives.
- Collaborate with local artists and storytellers to create narratives that inspire courage.

- Challenge and question cultural narratives that perpetuate unhealthy fears, fostering critical awareness.

3. Empowering Others through Compassionate Storytelling:

Overviews:
- Compassionate storytelling involves sharing experiences to foster understanding and empathy.
- Empowering others through storytelling creates a supportive community for facing fears together.
- The act of listening to others' stories contributes to a collective sense of resilience and connection.
- Compassionate storytelling is a reciprocal process, benefiting both the storyteller and the audience.
- Building a culture of compassionate storytelling reduces the stigma associated with fear.

Explorations:
- Explore the concept of empathy and its role in compassionate storytelling.
- Investigate how compassionate storytelling creates a safe space for vulnerability and healing.
- Examine the impact of shared stories in support groups or therapeutic settings.
- Understand the dynamics of active listening and its role in compassionate storytelling.
- Reflect on how your personal experiences can be shared to inspire and empower others.

Action Steps:
- Join or initiate a storytelling group focused on sharing and supporting each other in overcoming fears.
- Actively listen to others' stories without judgment, creating a non-judgmental space.
- Mentor or guide others in crafting and sharing their empowering narratives.
- Organize community events that highlight compassionate storytelling as a tool for resilience.
- Use digital platforms to share stories of triumph over fear, inspiring a broader audience.

4. Redefining Failure through Narratives:

Overviews:
- Failure is often stigmatized, but storytelling offers a chance to redefine its meaning.
- Personal narratives can shift the focus from fear of failure to embracing it as a part of growth.
- The stories we tell ourselves about failure shape our willingness to take risks and face fear.
- Narratives around failure impact self-esteem and the ability to bounce back from setbacks.
- Rewriting the narrative of failure allows individuals to approach challenges with resilience.

Explorations:
- Examine societal narratives around success and failure and their influence on individual fears.
- Reflect on personal stories of failure and how they have contributed to your growth.
- Explore narratives of well-known figures who have embraced failure as a stepping stone to success.
- Analyze the language used in failure narratives and its impact on self-perception.
- Understand how cultural narratives can stigmatize or celebrate failure.

Action Steps:
- Share your stories of failure with others, emphasizing the lessons learned and personal growth.
- Challenge societal norms around failure by promoting narratives that destigmatize it.
- Mentor individuals, emphasizing that failure is a natural part of the learning process.
- Create a "Failure Journal" to document and reflect on failures, fostering a growth mindset.
- Organize events or workshops that celebrate failure as a catalyst for resilience.

5. Future-focused Narratives: Creating a Fearless Tomorrow:

Overviews:
- Narratives about the future play a pivotal role in shaping our expectations, anxieties, and aspirations, influencing our outlook on what lies ahead.
- The fear of the unknown often stems from negative narratives about potential future outcomes, contributing to heightened anxiety and uncertainty.
- Crafting positive and empowering future narratives becomes instrumental in cultivating a fearless mindset, reshaping our anticipations towards optimism and resilience.
- Imagining a fearless future requires a conscious effort in shaping the stories we tell ourselves, redirecting the narrative focus from fear to empowerment.
- Future-focused narratives, when positive, instill hope, motivation, and a profound sense of agency, fostering the belief in one's capability to overcome future challenges.

Explorations:
- Explore personal narratives about the future, identifying patterns rooted in fear that may hinder the ability to approach the unknown with confidence.

- Reflect on how cultural and societal narratives influence individual and collective perceptions of the future, recognizing external factors shaping our outlook.
- Examine the role of imagination and creativity in crafting future-focused narratives, tapping into these faculties to create compelling and positive stories.
- Understand how past narratives, especially those linked to significant life events, contribute to current fears about the future, providing insights for narrative reconstruction.
- Investigate the correlation between positive future narratives and mental well-being, exploring how cultivating optimistic outlooks contributes to resilience.

Action Steps:
- Envision and articulate your ideal future in a written or visual format.
- Identify and challenge negative narratives about the future, replacing them with empowering ones.
- Collaborate with others to create a shared vision of a fearless future.
- Establish short-term goals aligned with your positive future narrative.
- Regularly revisit and revise your future-focused narrative, adapting it to evolving aspirations.

Chapter 17

Fear in Relationships:
Cultivating Secure Connections

1. Understanding the Dynamics of Fear in Relationships:
Overviews:
- Unpack the fundamental dynamics of fear within relationships, acknowledging its impact on individuals and the relationship as a whole.
- Recognize and comprehend the various triggers that induce fear in relationships, ranging from past traumas to current insecurities.
- Explore how fear manifests through communication patterns, influencing expressions of vulnerability, trust, and emotional intimacy.

Explorations:
- Encourage self-reflection on personal fears within the relationship, fostering awareness of how individual fears may contribute to relational dynamics.
- Promote open dialogues about fear between partners, creating a safe space for honest conversations about insecurities, expectations, and vulnerabilities.
- Delve into past experiences and how they shape present fears, encouraging a deeper understanding of each other's backgrounds.
- Engage in attachment style assessments, individually and as a couple, to gain insights into how attachment patterns may influence the experience of fear.

Action Steps:
- Invest in developing emotional regulation skills to manage fear-induced reactions, promoting healthier and more constructive responses.
- Collaboratively establish relationship goals that address individual and collective fears, fostering a shared vision for growth and connection.
- Develop a communication plan that encourages fear-free conversations, emphasizing active listening, empathy, and validation.
- Engage in joint activities that promote a sense of security and joy, enhancing the positive aspects of the relationship and counteracting fear.
- Schedule regular relationship check-ins to discuss fears, assess progress, and make necessary adjustments to relationship dynamics.

2. Nurturing Emotional Safety in Relationships:
Overviews:
- Establish emotional safety as the cornerstone of a healthy relationship, providing a secure environment for vulnerability and authenticity.
- Emphasize the importance of trust-building actions and behaviors to create a foundation where fear is minimized, and emotional safety is maximized.
- Explore the role of setting and respecting boundaries in cultivating emotional safety, ensuring that each partner feels valued and secure.
- Cultivate an atmosphere that encourages openness and transparency, allowing both partners to express fears without judgment.

Explorations:
- Encourage individuals to explore and communicate their personal comfort zones, fostering an understanding of each other's emotional needs.
- Reflect on past experiences of emotional safety and insecurity, identifying patterns and learning from both positive and challenging moments.
- Collaboratively define and work towards shared goals related to emotional safety, ensuring alignment in efforts to create a fear-free environment.
- Conduct a joint assessment of existing boundaries in the relationship, allowing for adjustments to enhance emotional safety.

- Understand individual emotional triggers and collaboratively develop strategies to navigate and overcome them.

Action Steps:
- Implement regular emotional check-ins to gauge the emotional well-being of each partner and address any emerging fears promptly.
- Consider couples therapy as a proactive measure to strengthen emotional safety, providing a structured space for facilitated discussions and growth.
- Engage in joint activities that promote personal and relational growth, reinforcing the positive aspects of the relationship.
- Foster a shared support system that extends beyond the relationship, creating additional layers of emotional security.
- Cultivate a habit of expressing appreciation for each other, reinforcing feelings of value and importance within the relationship.

3. Fostering Effective Communication:
Overviews:
- Recognize effective communication as a foundational element in mitigating fear and building understanding.
- Emphasize the importance of active listening, ensuring that both partners feel heard, understood, and validated.
- Prioritize clarity and transparency in communication, minimizing ambiguity and reducing the potential for misinterpretation and fear.
- Cultivate empathy as a key component of communication, allowing partners to connect emotionally and share in each other's experiences.
- Promote a culture of constructive feedback, where communication becomes a tool for growth and mutual support.

Explorations:
- Reflect on individual communication styles, identifying strengths, weaknesses, and potential areas for improvement.
- Understand the significance of non-verbal cues in communication and how they contribute to the overall emotional atmosphere.
- Review past instances of miscommunication, analyzing the root causes and exploring alternative approaches for better understanding.
- Explore and understand each other's love languages, facilitating more effective and meaningful communication.

Action Steps:
- Participate in communication skills workshops or seminars to enhance understanding and application of effective communication techniques.
- Implement regular relationship check-ins specifically dedicated to assessing and improving communication dynamics.
- Integrate mindfulness practices into communication, fostering a focused and present approach to discussions.
- Consider seeking therapeutic support, such as couples counseling, to address communication challenges and enhance relational dynamics.
- Develop shared communication goals, fostering a sense of unity in working towards improved and fear-free interactions.

4. Building Trust and Security:
Overviews:
- Acknowledge trust as a cornerstone of a fear-free relationship, establishing a sense of security and emotional safety.
- Highlight the importance of transparency and consistency in actions and communication to foster trust.
- Recognize that vulnerability is inherent in any relationship; develop strategies to navigate vulnerability with empathy and understanding.
- Understand the role of reliability in building security, where both partners can depend on each other consistently.

- Emphasize the capacity for forgiveness and repair as essential elements in rebuilding trust after conflicts.

Explorations:
- Reflect on past instances of trust-building or breaches, understanding the dynamics at play and identifying patterns.
- Examine individual thresholds for trust, recognizing how they may differ and working towards mutual understanding.
- Explore narratives around betrayal, acknowledging the impact, and working together on the path to recovery.
- Explore what emotional safety means for each partner and work collaboratively to create a safe and nurturing environment.
- Identify specific actions and behaviors that contribute to trust-building, fostering a shared commitment to their integration into the relationship.

Action Steps:
- Engage in trust-building exercises designed to enhance connection and confidence in each other.
- Prioritize open and honest conversations about expectations, boundaries, and shared values to strengthen trust.
- Consider seeking therapeutic interventions, such as trust-focused counseling, to navigate complex trust issues.
- Implement regular assessments of the relationship's trust dynamics, fostering ongoing improvement and growth.
- Establish a system of mutual accountability, where both partners actively contribute to building and maintaining trust.

5. Cultivating Shared Goals and Values:

Overviews:
- Recognize the importance of aligning long-term visions and goals to create a sense of shared purpose and direction.
- Understand shared values as anchors that provide stability and coherence, especially during challenging times.
- Highlight the significance of collaborative decision-making, ensuring both partners actively contribute to shaping their shared future.
- Emphasize the balance between individual growth and shared goals, allowing room for personal development within the relationship.

Explorations:
- Explore individual aspirations, discussing how they align with or complement each other within the context of the relationship.
- Reflect on core values that define personal identities and evaluate their resonance within the relationship.
- Discover shared interests and hobbies, providing opportunities for joint activities that contribute to mutual goals.
- Explore how differences in goals and values can be navigated, emphasizing understanding and compromise.

Action Steps:
- Schedule regular sessions for goal-setting and vision planning, ensuring both partners actively contribute to the process.
- Celebrate individual and shared milestones, reinforcing the sense of achievement and progress.
- Seek professional support, such as relationship coaching, to facilitate effective goal alignment and planning.
- Implement periodic relationship check-ins to assess the alignment of goals and make adjustments as needed.
- Actively engage in joint activities and initiatives that contribute to shared goals, deepening the connection and commitment to the relationship.

Chapter **18**

Fear at Work:
Overcoming Professional Insecurities

1. Acknowledging Professional Insecurities:
Overviews:
- Recognize that professional insecurities are common and experienced by many individuals in various workplace settings.
- Understand how unaddressed insecurities can impact job performance, job satisfaction, and overall well-being.
- Explore both external factors (work environment, colleagues) and internal factors (self-perception, imposter syndrome) contributing to professional insecurities.
- Recognize the intricate connection between fear and professional insecurities, often fueling a cycle of self-doubt and apprehension.

Explorations:
- Engage in introspection to identify specific professional insecurities and their origins.
- Explore how these insecurities affect job performance, relationships with colleagues, and overall career trajectory.
- Reflect on the role of external validation in mitigating or exacerbating professional insecurities.
- Examine how organizational culture and dynamics may contribute to or alleviate professional insecurities.

Action Steps:
- Establish a practice of regular journaling to delve into and process professional insecurities through self-reflection.
- Seek mentorship or guidance from colleagues, superiors, or mentors to gain insights and advice on overcoming specific insecurities.
- Actively pursue professional development opportunities to enhance skills and competencies, addressing areas contributing to insecurities.
- Request constructive feedback from supervisors and peers to gain a more accurate and balanced perspective on performance.
- Consider seeking therapeutic support, such as counseling or coaching, to address deeper-rooted insecurities and build resilience.
- Overcoming professional insecurities begins with acknowledging their existence, understanding their impact, and taking proactive steps towards self-improvement and confidence-building.

2. Creating a Positive Work Environment:
Overviews:
- Recognize the substantial impact of the work environment on individual well-being and professional confidence.
- Understand how a positive work environment contributes to increased job satisfaction and a sense of security.
- Emphasize the importance of healthy relationships with colleagues in fostering a positive and supportive workplace.
- Acknowledge the crucial role of leadership in shaping the overall work culture and environment.
- Highlight the significance of a culture that promotes continuous learning, growth, and collaboration.

Explorations:
- Assess the current workplace dynamics, identifying elements that contribute to a positive or negative environment.
- Explore how different leadership styles influence the overall work culture and employee confidence.
- Examine the level of collaboration and support within teams, recognizing its impact on individual confidence.
- Identify existing opportunities for skill development and professional growth within the organization.
- Evaluate the presence of programs or initiatives focused on employee well-being and mental health.

Action Steps:
- Encourage open communication with leadership to express concerns and suggestions for fostering a positive work environment.
- Initiate or participate in team-building activities to strengthen relationships and enhance collaboration.
- Advocate for the establishment of feedback channels where employees can share insights on the work environment.
- Actively participate in training and development programs to enhance skills and boost confidence.
- Support or champion initiatives related to mental health and well-being in the workplace.

3. Developing Resilience in the Face of Setbacks:

Overviews:
- Acknowledge that setbacks are inherent in professional life and can serve as opportunities for growth.
- Understand the importance of reframing failures as learning experiences rather than personal shortcomings.
- Emphasize the role of emotional resilience in bouncing back from setbacks and maintaining confidence.
- Recognize the need for self-compassion in the face of challenges, understanding that everyone experiences setbacks.
- Cultivate a long-term perspective, recognizing that setbacks are temporary and do not define one's entire professional journey.

Explorations:
- Reflect on past professional setbacks, analyzing the emotions and lessons associated with each experience.
- Explore personal strategies that have been effective in bouncing back from challenges in the past.
- Identify role models or individuals who exhibit resilience in the face of setbacks, learning from their approaches.
- Examine the current mindset towards setbacks and identify areas for a more resilient perspective.
- Explore the capacity to extract constructive feedback from setbacks, using criticism as a tool for improvement.

Action Steps:
- Incorporate resilience-building practices into daily routines, such as mindfulness, self-reflection, and gratitude.
- Actively seek out professional development opportunities that align with areas where setbacks have occurred.
- Cultivate a support network within the workplace, including mentors, colleagues, or friends who can provide guidance during challenging times.
- Developing resilience involves a proactive approach to setbacks, transforming them into opportunities for growth, learning, and enhanced professional confidence.

4. Navigating Workplace Competition and Comparison:

Overviews:
- Acknowledge the existence of competition in the workplace and its potential impact on individual confidence.
- Distinguish between healthy competition that motivates and unhealthy comparison that breeds insecurity.
- Emphasize the importance of individual growth rather than constant comparison to external benchmarks.
- Recognize the negative impact of constant comparison on mental well-being and professional confidence.
- Highlight the benefits of fostering a culture of collaboration and mutual support rather than intense competition.

Explorations:
- Engage in self-reflection to identify instances of feeling competitive and explore the emotions associated with such experiences.
- Explore personal motivations behind professional goals, distinguishing between intrinsic and extrinsic drivers.

- Reflect on the impact of comparing oneself to peers, considering how it influences confidence and overall job satisfaction.
- Examine the perception of success and whether it aligns with personal values or is influenced by external standards.
- Identify opportunities for collaboration with colleagues, emphasizing shared success and mutual support.

Action Steps:

- Practice mindfulness when feelings of competition arise, focusing on the present moment rather than future outcomes.
- Celebrate individual milestones and achievements, reinforcing a sense of accomplishment independent of others.
- Actively participate in collaborative projects or initiatives that foster teamwork and shared success.

5. Establishing Boundaries for Well-being:

Overviews:

- Recognize the essential role of establishing boundaries in maintaining overall well-being and professional confidence.
- Emphasize the importance of maintaining a balance between work commitments and personal life to prevent burnout.
- Understand that establishing boundaries is an act of self-respect, signaling personal limits to colleagues and superiors.
- Acknowledge that well-defined boundaries contribute to a sense of control and confidence in professional interactions.
- Recognize the role of a supportive work environment in respecting and accommodating individual boundaries.

- **Explorations:**

- Engage in self-reflection to assess the current state of work-life balance and the impact on overall well-being.
- Identify specific situations or tasks that contribute to stress and assess the need for boundaries in these areas.
- Explore ways to effectively communicate personal and professional limits to colleagues and superiors.
- Reflect on past instances of overcommitment and explore the consequences on mental health and professional confidence.
- Explore workplace practices that support the establishment and maintenance of healthy boundaries.

Action Steps:

- Define and communicate clear work hours, separating dedicated work time from personal time.
- Incorporate scheduled breaks into the workday to prevent burnout and promote mental well-being.
- Actively use allocated vacation time for rejuvenation and relaxation, avoiding the accumulation of unused days.
- Establish boundaries for after-work communication, ensuring designated periods of uninterrupted personal time.
- Reach out for support from colleagues or superiors when feeling overwhelmed, addressing challenges in maintaining boundaries.

Chapter 19

The Fear of Success:
Navigating Achievement Anxiety

1. Embracing the Fear of Success:
Overviews:
- Acknowledge that fear of success is a common phenomenon that can generate anxiety.
- Understand how the fear of success may hinder the pursuit of ambitious goals and aspirations.
- Recognize the paradoxical nature of fearing success, where achieving one's goals may evoke anxiety.
- Explore societal and cultural factors that contribute to the fear of success and its perception.
- Embrace the fear of success as an opportunity for personal growth and empowerment.

Explorations:
- Reflect on personal experiences and attitudes toward success, identifying moments of discomfort or anxiety.
- Investigate the origins of the fear of success, considering early experiences, societal expectations, or personal beliefs.
- Examine how the fear of success influences the setting of goals, potentially leading to self-sabotage.
- Explore the role of comparing oneself to others and societal expectations in fostering achievement anxiety.
- Understand recurring psychological patterns associated with the fear of success, such as imposter syndrome or fear of scrutiny.

Action Steps:
- Maintain a journal to document thoughts and emotions related to the fear of success, fostering self-awareness.
- Practice visualization exercises to imagine successful outcomes, gradually desensitizing the fear response.
- Develop positive affirmations to counteract negative beliefs about success, promoting a mindset of empowerment.
- Gradually expose oneself to success-related scenarios, challenging and reshaping the fear response.
- Seek guidance from a mentor, coach, or therapist to navigate and overcome the fear of success, benefiting from external perspectives.

2. Overcoming Perfectionism:
Overviews:
- Recognize perfectionism as a potential barrier to success, hindering progress and causing anxiety.
- Understand the distinction between striving for excellence and the unattainable pursuit of perfection.
- Acknowledge the negative impact of perfectionism on mental health, contributing to stress and fear.
- Explore the roots of perfectionistic traits, considering upbringing, societal pressure, or personal standards.
- Embrace a mindset shift that values progress, learning, and growth over unattainable perfection.

Explorations:
- Reflect on personal standards and expectations, evaluating whether they align with realistic goals.
- Explore the underlying fear associated with imperfection, recognizing it as a common human experience.
- Examine how perfectionism influences decision-making processes and the fear of making mistakes.
- Identify areas where perfectionism is particularly pronounced and assess its impact on overall well-being.
- Practice cognitive restructuring techniques to challenge and reframe perfectionistic thoughts and beliefs.

Action Steps:
- Establish realistic and achievable goals, breaking down larger objectives into manageable steps.

- Cultivate self-compassion through mindfulness and self-care practices, fostering a kinder attitude toward oneself.
- Embrace mistakes as opportunities for learning and growth, adopting a mindful approach to imperfections.
- Share goals and progress with a trusted friend or mentor, creating accountability and support in overcoming perfectionism.
- Maintain a journal to track perfectionistic tendencies, enhancing self-awareness and facilitating targeted interventions.

3. Fear of High Expectations:
Overviews:
- Recognize the potential negative impact of setting excessively high expectations on mental well-being.
- Understand the importance of balancing ambition with realistic expectations to manage fear.
- Differentiate between expectations imposed externally and those set internally, acknowledging personal agency.
- Explore the fear of disappointing others or oneself as a common element in the fear of high expectations.
- Embrace a mindset shift that views expectations as flexible, evolving with growth and learning.

Explorations:
- Reflect on personal expectations, evaluating their origins and influence on life decisions.
- Identify specific triggers that intensify the fear of high expectations, such as societal pressure or past experiences.
- Examine how the fear of high expectations affects persistence in pursuing long-term goals.
- Distinguish between healthy aspirations and unrealistic expectations, promoting a balanced approach.
- Investigate cultural norms and societal expectations regarding success and achievement, considering their impact on personal expectations.

Action Steps:
- Break down larger goals into realistic milestones, fostering a sense of achievement along the way.
- Schedule regular self-reflection sessions to assess alignment between expectations and personal values.
- Clearly communicate personal boundaries and limitations to manage external expectations effectively.
- Engage in collaborative goal-setting with mentors, colleagues, or family members to ensure alignment with personal values.
- Integrate mindfulness practices to stay present, manage expectations in the moment, and prevent future anxieties.

4. Fear of Evaluation and Judgment:
Overviews:
- Recognize the fear associated with evaluations, whether in professional, academic, or personal contexts.
- Understand how the fear of evaluation can influence self-esteem and confidence levels.
- Acknowledge that fear of evaluation is a common human experience, transcending individual circumstances.
- Explore the link between the fear of evaluation and broader social anxiety, identifying interconnected patterns.
- Recognize common coping mechanisms employed to manage the fear of evaluation, whether adaptive or maladaptive.

Explorations:
- Reflect on past experiences of evaluation, assessing emotional and cognitive responses.
- Identify specific situations or contexts that trigger fear of evaluation, uncovering patterns.
- Understand how the fear of evaluation is often intertwined with the fear of failure and its psychological implications.
- Examine how the fear of evaluation influences decision-making processes, potentially leading to avoidance behaviors.
- Explore cultural perspectives on evaluation and judgment, recognizing diverse views on success and failure.

Action Steps:

- Gradually expose oneself to evaluation scenarios, starting with less anxiety-inducing situations.
- Practice cognitive restructuring to challenge negative thoughts related to evaluation, fostering a more balanced perspective.
- Engage in positive visualization exercises to imagine successful outcomes in evaluation scenarios.
- Develop strategies for seeking constructive feedback, transforming evaluations into opportunities for growth.
- Cultivate a support system of friends, mentors, or colleagues who can provide encouragement and perspective during evaluation moments.

5. Fear of Rejection:

Overviews:

- Acknowledge that the fear of rejection is a universal human experience, transcending cultural and social boundaries.
- Understand how the fear of rejection can influence the formation and maintenance of interpersonal relationships.
- Explore the evolutionary roots of the fear of rejection and its adaptive significance in social contexts.
- Recognize the inherent vulnerability associated with the fear of rejection and its impact on emotional well-being.
- Embrace a shift from avoidance of rejection to acceptance of vulnerability as a courageous aspect of human connection.

Explorations:

- Reflect on personal experiences with rejection, identifying emotional and behavioral responses.
- Identify specific triggers that intensify the fear of rejection, such as social situations or personal insecurities.
- Examine how the fear of rejection may influence self-worth and self-perception in various life domains.
- Explore coping mechanisms used to manage the fear of rejection, recognizing their effectiveness and potential drawbacks.

Action Steps:

- Gradually expose oneself to situations that involve the possibility of rejection, building resilience over time.
- Practice self-compassion techniques to nurture a kind and understanding relationship with oneself, independent of external validation.
- Foster resilience in interpersonal relationships by embracing the possibility of rejection as part of the human experience.
- Develop effective communication skills to express thoughts, feelings, and boundaries, reducing the fear of rejection.
- Engage in community or social activities to broaden social connections and reduce the impact of individual rejection experiences.

Chapter 20

Social Fears and Public Life:
Finding Comfort in Community

1. Navigating Social Anxiety:
Overviews:
- Social fears are common, encompassing anxiety about social interactions, public speaking, and group settings.
- Understanding the roots of social anxiety involves exploring personal experiences, societal expectations, and the fear of judgment.
- Social fears can impact mental health, hinder professional growth, and limit the richness of personal relationships.
- The journey to finding comfort in community involves acknowledging social fears and developing strategies for effective navigation.
- Overcoming social anxiety contributes to a more fulfilling social life and increased overall well-being.

Explorations:
- Reflect on specific situations triggering social anxiety, examining associated thoughts and emotions.
- Explore the role of self-perception in social fears and its influence on interactions with others.
- Investigate societal norms and expectations related to social behavior, questioning their impact on personal comfort.
- Understand the physiological responses to social anxiety, recognizing patterns of fight-flight-freeze reactions.
- Examine the connection between social fears and self-esteem, recognizing the reciprocal influence.

Action Steps:
- Initiate gradual exposure to social situations, starting with smaller and more familiar settings.
- Challenge negative thought patterns related to social fears through cognitive restructuring techniques.
- Invest in enhancing social skills through workshops, courses, or self-directed learning.
- Build a support network of understanding friends or mentors to share experiences and seek guidance.
- Consider seeking professional help, such as therapy, to address deep-seated social anxieties.

2. Embracing Authenticity in Social Settings:
Overviews:
- Authenticity involves being true to oneself in social interactions, free from excessive concern about external judgment.
- Finding comfort in community is intricately linked to the ability to express authenticity without fear of rejection.
- Authenticity fosters genuine connections, mutual understanding, and a sense of belonging in social circles.
- Overcoming the fear of judgment is a key aspect of embracing authenticity in various social settings.
- The journey towards authenticity requires self-discovery, self-acceptance, and a willingness to be vulnerable.

Explorations:
- Reflect on personal values, interests, and beliefs, exploring how they align with social behaviors.
- Examine past experiences where authenticity led to positive connections and enhanced relationships.
- Investigate societal norms that may hinder authentic expression, questioning their impact on personal well-being.
- Understand the role of vulnerability in authentic interactions, recognizing its power in building connections.
- Explore the concept of self-compassion and its role in overcoming the fear of judgment in social settings.

Action Steps:
- Engage in self-discovery practices, such as journaling or mindfulness, to understand personal values.

- Begin expressing authenticity gradually in low-stakes situations, building confidence over time.
- Establish clear personal boundaries, ensuring a balance between authenticity and self-protection.
- Solicit feedback from trusted individuals on authentic expressions, fostering growth and refinement.
- Cultivate self-compassion as a tool to navigate challenges and setbacks on the journey to authenticity.

3. Building Social Resilience:

Overviews:
- Social resilience involves the ability to adapt and bounce back from social challenges and setbacks.
- Developing social resilience contributes to increased confidence, improved interpersonal skills, and a more positive outlook on social interactions.
- Recognizing that occasional social discomfort is a natural part of growth and learning in social settings.
- Overcoming the fear of failure or embarrassment is crucial for building social resilience.
- Social resilience extends beyond individual experiences, contributing to the overall well-being of communities.

Explorations:
- Reflect on past social challenges and identify lessons learned, acknowledging personal growth.
- Examine the role of mindset in shaping responses to social setbacks, exploring the potential for a growth-oriented perspective.
- Investigate the connection between self-compassion and social resilience, recognizing their symbiotic relationship.
- Explore diverse cultural perspectives on social resilience, understanding how different societies navigate social challenges.
- Understand the dynamics of group resilience, recognizing the supportive role of communities in overcoming social fears.

Action Steps:
- Integrate positive affirmations into daily routines to foster a resilient mindset in social situations.
- View social setbacks as opportunities for learning and growth, reframing negative experiences.
- Actively participate in community activities or groups to broaden social exposure and build resilience.
- Incorporate mindfulness practices to stay present in social interactions, reducing anticipatory anxiety.
- Establish mentorship or seek guidance from individuals experienced in navigating social challenges, learning from their insights.

4. Effective Communication Strategies:

Overviews:
- Effective communication is foundational to successful social interactions and the reduction of social fears.
- Building communication skills involves verbal and non-verbal cues, active listening, and empathy.
- Fear of miscommunication or being misunderstood can contribute to social anxiety and inhibitions.
- Recognizing the role of assertiveness in clear and authentic communication, free from passive or aggressive tendencies.
- Effective communication fosters understanding, strengthens relationships, and reduces social apprehensions.

Explorations:
- Reflect on past communication experiences and identify patterns of successful and challenging interactions.
- Explore cultural nuances in communication, recognizing the impact of diverse communication styles.
- Investigate the connection between self-esteem and communication effectiveness, understanding their interplay.
- Understand the dynamics of non-verbal communication, exploring its role in conveying emotions and intentions.
- Examine assertiveness techniques and their application in expressing needs and boundaries authentically.

Action Steps:
- Attend communication workshops or courses to enhance verbal and non-verbal communication skills.
- Cultivate active listening skills, ensuring a deeper understanding of others in social interactions.
- Engage in role-playing scenarios to practice assertiveness and effective communication.

- Solicit constructive feedback on communication from peers or mentors to identify areas for improvement.
- Maintain a communication journal to reflect on daily interactions, noting successes and areas for growth.

5. Community Engagement:

Overviews:
- Active participation in community activities enhances social connections and reduces individual fears.
- Communities provide a supportive environment for personal and collective growth, fostering a sense of belonging.
- Shared experiences within communities contribute to a sense of understanding and empathy, reducing social anxieties.
- Building a sense of community involves finding like-minded individuals with common interests or goals.
- Community engagement extends beyond personal comfort zones, encouraging exploration and diverse social connections.

Explorations:
- Reflect on past community experiences and identify the positive impact on social well-being.
- Explore various communities, both online and offline, recognizing the diversity of social connections available.
- Investigate the role of community norms in shaping individual behaviors and alleviating social fears.
- Understand the potential for personal growth within communities, acknowledging the reciprocal nature of support.
- Examine the impact of community engagement on mental health and overall life satisfaction.

Action Steps:
- Identify personal interests or passions that align with potential community engagements.
- Attend local meetups, events, or online groups to connect with individuals who share similar interests.
- Explore volunteer opportunities within communities to contribute while building connections.
- Actively participate in community discussions, events, or collaborative projects to enhance involvement.
- Offer support and encouragement to fellow community members, fostering a positive and reciprocal atmosphere.

Chapter 21

The Fear of Unknown:
Embracing Uncertainty

1. Embracing Uncertainty as a Natural State:
Overviews:
- Uncertainty is an inherent aspect of life, and the fear of the unknown is a common human experience.
- Recognizing uncertainty as a natural state allows for a shift in perspective, fostering adaptability and resilience.
- Fear of the unknown often stems from a desire for control, and embracing uncertainty involves letting go of the need for absolute certainty.
- The ability to navigate uncertain situations is a valuable skill that contributes to personal growth and well-being.
- Embracing uncertainty is not about eliminating fear but learning to coexist with it while moving forward.

Explorations:
- Reflect on past experiences of uncertainty and how they contributed to personal growth.
- Explore the cultural and societal influences on perceptions of uncertainty and fear of the unknown.
- Investigate the physiological responses to uncertainty, understanding the mind-body connection.
- Examine the role of mindfulness in cultivating acceptance of uncertainty and reducing anxiety.
- Understand the concept of radical acceptance, acknowledging that some aspects of life are beyond control.

Action Steps:
- Incorporate mindfulness practices, such as meditation, to build resilience in the face of uncertainty.
- Gradually expose yourself to controlled uncertain situations, building tolerance over time.
- Maintain a journal to record thoughts and emotions related to uncertainty, fostering self-awareness.
- Share uncertainties with trusted friends or a therapist, gaining diverse perspectives and support.
- Reflect on past uncertain experiences, extracting lessons and growth opportunities.

2. Cultivating a Positive Relationship with Ambiguity:
Overviews:
- Ambiguity often accompanies uncertainty, and developing a positive relationship with ambiguity is key to overcoming fear.
- Embracing ambiguity involves reframing it as an opportunity for creativity, exploration, and learning.
- Fear of the unknown can be mitigated by viewing ambiguity as a space for potential growth and discovery.
- A positive relationship with ambiguity contributes to increased adaptability and a willingness to embrace new opportunities.
- The journey to cultivate positivity towards ambiguity requires a mindset shift and intentional practice.

Explorations:
- Reflect on personal reactions to ambiguity, identifying patterns of resistance or openness.
- Explore the connection between fear of ambiguity and perfectionism, understanding the desire for clear answers.
- Investigate how cultural perspectives influence attitudes towards ambiguity and the unknown.
- Examine historical examples of individuals or societies embracing ambiguity and achieving innovation or progress.
- Understand the psychological benefits of curiosity and its role in fostering a positive relationship with ambiguity.

Action Steps:
- Intentionally shift your mindset towards ambiguity, viewing it as an opportunity rather than a threat.
- Engage in creative exercises or hobbies that involve navigating uncertain or ambiguous situations.

- Challenge perfectionistic tendencies by accepting imperfections and uncertainties in various aspects of life.
- Cultivate curiosity by exploring new interests, ideas, or perspectives, fostering a sense of wonder.
- Incorporate positive affirmations that reinforce the idea that ambiguity is a source of growth and learning.

3. Building Resilience in the Face of Uncertainty:

Overviews:
- Resilience plays a crucial role in navigating uncertainty, allowing individuals to bounce back from challenges.
- Building resilience involves developing coping mechanisms, adaptive strategies, and a mindset that fosters perseverance.
- Uncertainty can be seen as an opportunity to build resilience, enhancing the ability to withstand and learn from unpredictable situations.
- Resilience in uncertainty contributes to increased emotional well-being and a more positive outlook on life.
- The journey to build resilience involves intentional efforts and a commitment to personal development.

Explorations:
- Reflect on past experiences of uncertainty and identify coping mechanisms that were effective.
- Explore the role of self-compassion in building resilience, acknowledging that navigating uncertainty is a shared human experience.
- Investigate the connection between adaptability and resilience, recognizing their intertwined nature in uncertain circumstances.
- Examine cultural perspectives on resilience, understanding how different societies approach and cultivate resilience.
- Understand the concept of post-traumatic growth and its relevance in the context of resilience amidst uncertainty.

Action Steps:
- Engage in resilience-building activities or workshops to enhance coping skills.
- Create a personalized resilience plan that includes coping strategies for various uncertain scenarios.
- Incorporate mind-body practices such as yoga or tai chi to enhance overall resilience.
- Seek mentorship from individuals who have demonstrated resilience in the face of uncertainty.
- Acknowledge and celebrate small achievements in navigating uncertain situations, fostering a positive feedback loop.

4. Mindfulness in Uncertain Moments:

Overviews:
- Mindfulness is a powerful tool for managing the fear of the unknown, grounding individuals in the present moment.
- Practicing mindfulness allows for a non-judgmental awareness of thoughts and emotions, reducing reactivity to uncertainty.
- Mindfulness fosters a sense of calm and acceptance, mitigating the anxiety often associated with unknown outcomes.
- The integration of mindfulness in daily life contributes to an overall sense of well-being and resilience.
- Cultivating mindfulness involves both formal practices and incorporating mindful moments into everyday activities.

Explorations:
- Reflect on past experiences where mindfulness or lack thereof influenced responses to uncertainty.
- Explore different mindfulness practices, such as meditation, mindful breathing, or body scan exercises, to identify preferences.
- Investigate the impact of mindfulness on cognitive processes, recognizing its ability to enhance focus and clarity in uncertain situations.
- Examine the role of mindfulness in reducing anticipatory anxiety, allowing individuals to approach the unknown with greater ease.
- Understand the connection between mindfulness and emotional regulation, particularly in the context of uncertainty.

- **Action Steps:**
  - Establish a daily mindfulness routine, incorporating practices into morning or evening rituals.
  - Introduce mindful moments throughout the day, such as mindful breathing during transitions or routine activities.
  - Practice mindful eating, savoring each bite and paying attention to the sensory experience during meals.
  - Explore mindfulness apps that offer guided sessions and support in developing a consistent practice.
  - Apply mindfulness techniques when making decisions, allowing for a more grounded and thoughtful approach.

5. Nurturing a Growth Mindset:

Overviews:
- A growth mindset is instrumental in facing uncertainty, as it emphasizes learning, resilience, and the potential for personal development.
- Individuals with a growth mindset perceive challenges as opportunities for growth rather than insurmountable obstacles.
- Cultivating a growth mindset involves reframing failures and setbacks as part of the learning journey.
- The fear of the unknown diminishes as a growth mindset fosters curiosity, adaptability, and a belief in one's capacity to learn.
- Nurturing a growth mindset contributes to increased confidence and a willingness to explore new and uncertain paths.

Explorations:
- Reflect on personal beliefs about learning and abilities, identifying fixed mindset tendencies.
- Explore the impact of societal expectations and educational systems on the development of a growth mindset.
- Investigate the relationship between a growth mindset and resilience, recognizing their interconnected nature.
- Examine historical or personal examples of individuals who embraced a growth mindset in the face of uncertainty.
- Understand the role of self-talk in nurturing a growth mindset, identifying and challenging limiting beliefs.

Action Steps:
- Engage in regular self-reflection to identify and challenge fixed mindset thoughts.
- Set specific learning goals that involve stepping out of comfort zones and embracing uncertainty.
- Cultivate a positive attitude towards failure, viewing it as a stepping stone to growth.
- Seek environments that encourage learning, experimentation, and continuous improvement.
- Embrace practices that support a learning mindset, such as seeking feedback, asking questions, and staying open to new experiences.

Chapter **22**

Fear and Finances:
Tackling Money-Related Worries

1. Understanding the Dynamics of Financial Fear:
Overviews:
- Financial fear encompasses a range of emotions tied to money, including anxiety, stress, and uncertainty.
- Exploring the root causes of financial fear involves understanding personal beliefs, societal expectations, and past experiences.
- Financial fear can impact mental well-being, relationships, and overall quality of life.
- Recognizing the commonality of financial fears reduces isolation and fosters a proactive approach to addressing concerns.
- An in-depth understanding of the dynamics of financial fear is crucial for developing effective strategies for financial well-being.

Explorations:
- Reflect on personal experiences and emotions related to money, identifying specific triggers for financial fear.
- Explore cultural and societal influences on attitudes towards money, acknowledging external pressures and expectations.
- Investigate how childhood experiences and family beliefs about money contribute to current financial fears.
- Examine the impact of media and societal narratives on perceptions of financial success and failure.
- Understand the psychological effects of financial fear on decision-making, risk-taking, and overall mental health.

Action Steps:
- Engage in a comprehensive financial self-assessment, including income, expenses, debts, and financial goals.
- Set achievable and realistic financial goals, breaking them down into manageable steps.
- Develop and maintain a budget to gain a clear understanding of income, expenses, and spending habits.
- Invest time in learning about personal finance, seeking guidance from financial advisors, books, or online resources.
- Consider seeking therapy or counseling to explore and address the emotional aspects of financial fears.

2. Building a Healthy Relationship with Money:
Overviews:
- A healthy relationship with money involves balancing financial responsibility, satisfaction, and well-being.
- Understanding personal values and priorities is foundational for developing a positive relationship with money.
- Building financial literacy and skills contributes to a sense of control and empowerment in managing money.
- Shifting focus from accumulating wealth for its own sake to aligning financial choices with personal values fosters contentment.
- A healthy relationship with money is an ongoing process of self-discovery, learning, and adapting to life changes.

Explorations:
- Reflect on personal values and how they align with current financial choices and behaviors.
- Explore different approaches to financial management, recognizing the importance of balance and flexibility.
- Investigate the role of materialism in shaping financial goals and assess its impact on overall well-being.

- Examine the connection between self-worth and financial success, challenging any negative associations.
- Understand the link between gratitude, contentment, and financial well-being.

Action Steps:
- Clearly define personal values and priorities to guide financial decisions.
- Invest time in ongoing financial education to enhance money management skills.
- Practice mindful spending by aligning purchases with values and long-term goals.
- Establish a routine for regular financial check-ins to assess progress and make adjustments.
- Seek guidance from financial planners or advisors to create a personalized financial plan.

3. Overcoming Debt-Related Anxiety:

Overviews:
- Debt-related anxiety is a common manifestation of financial fear, impacting mental health and overall well-being.
- Understanding the psychological effects of debt involves acknowledging shame, guilt, and stress associated with owing money.
- Overcoming debt-related anxiety requires a strategic approach that combines financial planning and emotional well-being.
- Breaking the cycle of debt involves addressing root causes, creating a sustainable repayment plan, and fostering a positive mindset.
- Reducing debt-related anxiety contributes to improved mental health and allows individuals to focus on long-term financial goals.

Explorations:
- Reflect on emotional responses to debt, identifying underlying beliefs and attitudes.
- Explore the connection between debt, self-worth, and social expectations, recognizing societal influences on perceptions of financial success.
- Investigate debt repayment strategies, considering both practical and emotional aspects of the process.
- Examine the impact of debt on mental health, relationships, and overall life satisfaction.
- Understand the role of self-compassion in overcoming debt-related anxiety and building a positive financial future.

Action Steps:
- Conduct a thorough assessment of current debts, interest rates, and repayment terms.
- Develop a prioritized plan for debt repayment, focusing on high-interest debts first.
- Adjust the budget to allocate specific funds for debt repayment while maintaining essential expenses.
- Seek guidance from financial counselors or debt management professionals for personalized strategies.
- Engage in open conversations about debt-related anxiety with trusted friends, family, or mental health professionals.

4. Investing and the Fear of Risk:

Overviews:
- The fear of financial risk often hinders individuals from engaging in investment opportunities that could lead to wealth accumulation.
- Understanding the psychology of risk involves assessing risk tolerance, acknowledging biases, and recognizing the impact of emotions on investment decisions.
- Overcoming the fear of financial risk requires a balanced approach that combines education, realistic expectations, and a well-defined investment strategy.
- Investing is a long-term endeavor, and embracing a strategic approach helps individuals navigate market fluctuations and uncertainties.
- Building confidence in investment decisions involves continuous learning, staying informed, and seeking professional advice when needed.

Explorations:
- Reflect on past experiences with investments, identifying emotional responses to market fluctuations.
- Explore the concept of risk tolerance and how individual risk preferences impact investment decisions.
- Investigate common cognitive biases that influence financial decision-making, particularly in the realm of investments.
- Examine the role of financial media in shaping perceptions of risk and its impact on investment behavior.

Action Steps:
- Evaluate personal risk tolerance and align investment choices accordingly.
- Build a diversified investment portfolio to spread risk and enhance long-term stability.
- Continuously educate yourself about investment principles, market trends, and financial instruments.
- Consult with financial advisors for personalized investment advice aligned with your financial goals.

5. Planning for the Future:

Overviews:
- Fear of an uncertain financial future can significantly impact present well-being, highlighting the importance of long-term planning.
- Future financial planning involves setting goals, creating emergency funds, and making informed decisions to ensure financial security.
- Overcoming the fear of the financial future requires a proactive approach that includes both short-term and long-term strategies.
- Financial planning empowers individuals to face uncertainties with resilience, providing a sense of control over their financial destiny.

Explorations:
- Reflect on current financial goals and aspirations, considering both short-term and long-term objectives.
- Explore the concept of financial resilience and how it contributes to facing future uncertainties.
- Investigate the role of emergency funds in providing a financial safety net and reducing anxiety about unexpected expenses.
- Examine the psychological benefits of setting and achieving financial goals for long-term well-being.

Action Steps:
- Define clear financial goals for different time horizons, considering immediate needs and long-term aspirations.
- Establish and regularly contribute to an emergency fund to cover unexpected expenses.
- Create a comprehensive financial plan that includes budgeting, investments, and retirement savings.
- Conduct regular reviews of financial goals and adjust plans based on changing circumstances.

Chapter 23

The Adventurer's Mindset:
Fear as a Catalyst for Growth

1. Embracing Fear as a Catalyst for Growth:
Overviews:
- Fear, when reframed, becomes a powerful catalyst for personal and professional growth.
- The adventurer's mindset views fear as a natural part of the journey, offering opportunities for resilience and learning.
- Embracing fear as a catalyst involves shifting from avoidance to curiosity and leveraging discomfort for transformative experiences.
- Recognizing the distinction between harmful fear and fear that propels growth is crucial for cultivating the adventurer's mindset.
- The integration of fear as a growth catalyst contributes to enhanced self-efficacy, adaptability, and a fulfilling life journey.

Explorations:
- Reflect on past experiences where fear acted as a catalyst for positive change or personal development.
- Explore cultural narratives around fear and growth, identifying societal influences on perceptions of discomfort.
- Examine the role of mindset in shaping reactions to fear, distinguishing between fixed and growth-oriented perspectives.
- Investigate stories of renowned adventurers or individuals who turned fear into a catalyst for significant achievements.
- Understand the physiological and psychological mechanisms that occur when fear is reframed as a tool for growth.

Action Steps:
- Maintain a fear journal to document instances where fear led to growth and positive outcomes.
- Engage in mindset training exercises to foster a growth-oriented perspective towards challenges.
- Gradually expose yourself to controlled levels of discomfort, expanding your comfort zone.
- Actively seek out challenges or adventures that evoke a sense of fear, embracing them as opportunities for growth.
- Celebrate small victories and personal growth achievements, reinforcing the positive connection between fear and advancement.

2. Cultivating Resilience in the Face of Fear:
Overviews:
- Resilience is a fundamental attribute of the adventurer's mindset, allowing individuals to bounce back from adversity.
- Cultivating resilience involves developing coping mechanisms, adaptive strategies, and a positive outlook in the presence of fear.
- Resilience enables individuals to navigate uncertainties, setbacks, and challenges with greater ease and determination.
- The adventurer's resilience is rooted in the understanding that setbacks are integral to the journey of growth.
- Building resilience in the face of fear contributes to mental fortitude, emotional well-being, and sustained personal development.

Explorations:
- Reflect on personal experiences of overcoming challenges, identifying resilience-building elements.
- Explore the connection between resilience, self-compassion, and the ability to face fear without succumbing to it.
- Examine the role of support systems and relationships in fostering resilience during times of fear.
- Investigate different resilience-building practices, such as mindfulness, gratitude, and goal-setting.

- Understand the impact of mindset on resilience, distinguishing between fixed and growth-oriented perspectives.

Action Steps:
- Engage in resilience-building exercises, including mindfulness practices and positive affirmations.
- Cultivate a network of supportive relationships to provide encouragement during challenging times.
- Regularly engage in activities that challenge your comfort zones, gradually increasing difficulty.
- Practice mindful reflection on setbacks, focusing on lessons learned and opportunities for growth.
- Maintain a resilience journal, recording instances where resilience was demonstrated, and lessons extracted.

3. Harnessing Fear for Creativity and Innovation:

Overviews:
- Fear can serve as a catalyst for creativity and innovation, inspiring novel solutions and unconventional thinking.
- The adventurer's mindset embraces fear-induced discomfort as a precursor to breakthrough ideas and unique perspectives.
- Recognizing fear's role in the creative process involves reframing it from an obstacle to a stimulus for original thinking.
- Creativity born from fear is often transformative, leading to innovative problem-solving and personal growth.
- Cultivating an environment that encourages the positive influence of fear on creativity enhances both professional and personal endeavors.

Explorations:
- Reflect on instances where fear stimulated creative thinking and problem-solving.
- Explore the historical and contemporary contributions of individuals who turned fear into a source of creative inspiration.
- Examine the connection between fear, risk-taking, and the generation of novel ideas.
- Investigate how diverse perspectives and experiences of fear contribute to a richer creative landscape.
- Understand the psychological mechanisms that link fear to enhanced cognitive flexibility and innovation.

Action Steps:
- Engage in creative challenges that involve stepping into unfamiliar or discomforting territory.
- Use mind mapping techniques to explore associations between fear, creativity, and potential solutions.
- Foster collaborative environments that value diverse perspectives, encouraging creative discussions.
- Initiate projects or endeavors that are driven by a healthy level of fear, pushing the boundaries of conventional thinking.
- Embrace a mindset of continuous learning, staying curious and open to new ideas, even in the face of uncertainty.

4. Fear as a Motivational Force:

Overviews:
- The adventurer's mindset views fear as a motivational force capable of propelling individuals towards meaningful goals.
- Fear, when channeled effectively, serves as a dynamic energy source for increased focus, determination, and persistence.
- Understanding the motivating power of fear involves discerning between paralyzing anxiety and the energizing drive to overcome challenges.
- Motivation derived from fear is sustainable when aligned with personal values and aspirations.
- Embracing fear as a motivational force fosters a proactive approach to goal-setting and achievement.

Explorations:
- Reflect on personal experiences where fear acted as a motivator, driving positive actions and achievements.
- Explore motivational theories related to fear, distinguishing between extrinsic and intrinsic sources of drive.
- Examine the impact of fear-induced motivation on goal clarity, persistence, and overall satisfaction.
- Investigate the role of mindset in transforming fear from an impediment to a catalyst for meaningful endeavors.

- Understand the balance between fear-driven motivation and the importance of self-care to prevent burnout.

Action Steps:
- Align personal and professional goals with intrinsic motivations, ensuring a meaningful connection to values.
- Use visualization techniques to imagine the positive outcomes and personal growth resulting from overcoming fear.
- Break down larger goals into actionable steps, turning fear-induced motivation into a series of manageable tasks.
- Establish accountability partnerships to share goals, progress, and provide mutual support.
- Regularly reflect on the motivational aspects of fear, acknowledging achievements and adapting strategies as needed.

5. Fear in Relationships: Navigating Interpersonal Challenges:

Overviews:
- Interpersonal relationships often evoke fear, requiring emotional intelligence and effective communication for resolution.
- The adventurer's mindset in relationships involves viewing conflicts and challenges as opportunities for mutual growth.
- Navigating fear in relationships necessitates empathy, active listening, and the ability to express vulnerability.
- Fear can either hinder or strengthen relationships, depending on how it is acknowledged and addressed.
- Cultivating an adventurer's mindset in relationships fosters resilience, trust, and shared personal development.

Explorations:
- Reflect on past relational conflicts and identify the role of fear in communication and understanding.
- Explore different communication styles and their impact on addressing fear-related issues in relationships.
- Examine cultural and societal influences on fear within relationships and their implications for interpersonal dynamics.
- Investigate successful relationship narratives where fear became a catalyst for deeper connection and understanding.
- Understand the reciprocal nature of fear in relationships, recognizing its impact on both individuals and the relationship dynamic.

Action Steps:
- Foster open and honest communication within relationships, addressing fears and concerns directly.
- Practice empathetic listening to understand the fears and perspectives of others in the relationship.
- Encourage vulnerability by sharing personal fears and concerns, fostering a deeper connection.
- Develop conflict resolution skills, including negotiation and compromise, to address fear-induced conflicts.
- Collaboratively create growth plans with individuals in the relationship, emphasizing shared goals and mutual support.

Chapter **24**

Creativity's Antidote to Fear:
Using Art to Heal

1. The Therapeutic Power of Art:
Overviews:

- Art serves as a transformative medium, offering a unique and expressive outlet for processing and healing from fear.
- Engaging in artistic endeavors activates various parts of the brain, contributing to emotional regulation and self-discovery.
- Creativity provides a non-linear approach to understanding and confronting fear, often unveiling insights that words alone cannot convey.
- Artistic expression facilitates catharsis, allowing individuals to release and make sense of complex emotions related to fear.
- Recognizing art as a therapeutic tool empowers individuals to embark on a healing journey with flexibility and self-compassion.

Explorations:

- Reflect on personal experiences with art as a means of emotional expression and its impact on mood.
- Explore different forms of artistic expression (visual arts, writing, music) and their potential in addressing fear.
- Examine the role of symbolism in art, understanding how it can represent and transform the experience of fear.
- Investigate art therapy modalities and their application in mental health treatment for fear-related challenges.
- Understand cross-cultural perspectives on art as a healing tool and its historical significance in various societies.

Action Steps:

- Experiment with different artistic mediums, allowing for the exploration of what resonates personally.
- Establish a routine for daily artistic expression, creating a consistent outlet for emotional release.
- Use art to symbolically represent fears, transforming them into tangible and manageable entities.
- Maintain an art journal to document thoughts, emotions, and artistic creations related to fear.
- Consider participating in formal art therapy sessions to receive professional guidance and support.

2. Narrative Healing Through Writing:
Overviews:

- Writing serves as a powerful tool for narrative healing, allowing individuals to construct and reconstruct their relationship with fear.
- The process of writing helps organize thoughts, gain clarity, and create a coherent narrative around fear-related experiences.
- Expressive writing has been linked to improved emotional well-being, reduced stress, and enhanced resilience.
- Through storytelling, individuals can redefine their experiences, reclaim agency, and foster a sense of authorship over their fear narratives.
- Recognizing writing as a form of therapeutic self-discovery enables a dynamic exploration of fears and personal growth.

Explorations:

- Reflect on personal experiences with writing as a means of processing fear and its impact on emotional well-being.
- Explore various writing techniques, such as journaling, poetry, or storytelling, and their effectiveness in addressing fear.
- Examine the connection between language, self-perception, and the construction of fear narratives.
- Investigate autobiographical writing and its role in reshaping one's life story in the context of fear.

- Understand the role of mindfulness in writing, fostering awareness and acceptance of fear-related thoughts and feelings.

Action Steps:
- Establish a daily journaling practice to reflect on fears, emotions, and personal insights.
- Engage in creative writing exercises that prompt exploration of fears from different angles.
- Experiment with poetry as a form of emotional expression, using metaphors and symbolism.
- Rewrite fear-related narratives, emphasizing resilience, growth, and lessons learned.
- Join writing workshops or groups to share experiences, gain feedback, and foster a sense of community.

3. The Therapeutic Soundscape:

Overviews:
- Sound and music provide a therapeutic avenue for emotional expression and regulation, offering a holistic approach to healing from fear.
- Engaging with sound activates the limbic system, influencing emotions and contributing to relaxation and stress reduction.
- Music, in particular, has the power to evoke and transform emotions, providing a safe space to explore and confront fear.
- Creating or listening to a curated soundscape allows individuals to tailor their auditory experience for emotional release and comfort.
- Recognizing the therapeutic potential of sound encourages the integration of music and intentional listening into fear-healing practices.

Explorations:
- Reflect on personal experiences with music or sound that have influenced emotional states related to fear.
- Explore different genres, instruments, and sounds to identify those that resonate positively during fear-inducing moments.
- Examine the connection between rhythm, tempo, and emotional arousal, understanding their impact on fear responses.
- Investigate the use of soundscapes, binaural beats, or guided meditation audio for fear-related relaxation and coping.
- Understand the cultural and historical significance of music and sound in rituals and healing practices.

Action Steps:
- Create playlists tailored to different emotional states, including calming and empowering music.
- Practice intentional listening, focusing on the nuances of sound, whether through music, nature sounds, or ambient noise.
- Experiment with creating soundscapes or playing musical instruments as a form of emotional release.
- Explore guided meditation sessions that incorporate therapeutic sounds for relaxation.
- Attend concerts, explore new music genres, and incorporate musical experiences into fear-healing routines.

4. Movement as Expression: Dance and Yoga:

Overviews:
- Movement-based practices such as dance and yoga offer embodied expressions of emotions, including those related to fear.
- Physical movement has been linked to improved mental well-being, stress reduction, and the release of endorphins.
- Dance allows for a non-verbal exploration of emotions, while yoga integrates movement with mindfulness and breath awareness.
- Mindful movement practices contribute to a sense of grounding, fostering resilience in the face of fear.
- Recognizing the body-mind connection in movement highlights the potential for transformative and healing experiences.

Explorations:
- Reflect on personal experiences with dance or yoga as outlets for emotional expression and stress relief.
- Explore different dance styles and yoga practices, considering their impact on emotional regulation and fear responses.

- Examine the role of breath in movement practices, understanding its connection to emotional states.
- Investigate the use of dance or yoga in therapeutic settings, such as dance/movement therapy or trauma-informed yoga.
- Understand the cultural and historical significance of dance and movement in rituals and healing practices.

Action Steps:
- Establish a routine that incorporates mindful movement, whether through dance or yoga.
- Engage in exploratory dance sessions to express emotions freely and without judgment.
- Explore yoga sequences designed for emotional release, focusing on postures that target fear-related tension.
- Join group dance or yoga classes for a sense of community and shared movement experiences.
- Practice body scan techniques during movement, cultivating awareness of physical sensations and emotions.

5. Externalizing Fear: Visual Arts and Sculpture:

Overviews:
- Externalizing fear through visual arts and sculpture provides a tangible and external representation of internal experiences.
- Creating visual representations of fear allows for a symbolic and transformative process of understanding and confronting it.
- Sculpture and visual arts offer a non-verbal means of communication, enabling individuals to express complex emotions.
- The act of creating visual art fosters a sense of agency and control over fear, promoting empowerment and resilience.

Explorations:
- Reflect on personal experiences with visual arts or sculpture as a means of externalizing and processing fear.
- Explore different art mediums, such as painting, drawing, or sculpting, and their impact on the expression of fear.
- Examine the symbolism and metaphorical aspects of visual representations of fear, considering cultural and personal influences.
- Investigate art therapy techniques that involve externalizing and transforming fear through visual arts.

Action Steps:
- Experiment with different visual art mediums, discovering those that resonate with the expression of fear.
- Create sculptures or three-dimensional representations symbolizing aspects of fear.
- Maintain a visual journal to document the evolution of visual representations of fear over time.
- Incorporate artistic rituals into fear-healing routines, using visual arts as a transformative tool.
- Join art exhibitions or groups to share and discuss visual representations of fear, fostering community and mutual support.

Chapter **25**

Technology Tools:
Apps and Resources for Fear Management

1. Overview of Technology in Fear Management:
Overviews:
- Technology tools, including apps and online resources, offer accessible and versatile means for managing and overcoming fear.
- These tools leverage various approaches, from mindfulness and cognitive-behavioral techniques to community support and educational resources.
- Integrating technology into fear management provides individuals with on-the-go and personalized solutions.
- Apps and resources often cater to diverse fear types, addressing specific needs and preferences.
- The use of technology enhances the democratization of mental health resources, making support available to a broader audience.

Explorations:
- Explore different fear management apps and platforms available for mobile devices and online access.
- Investigate the methodologies and therapeutic approaches employed by these technological tools in addressing fear.
- Examine user reviews and testimonials to understand real-world experiences and effectiveness.
- Understand the privacy and security features of fear management apps to ensure confidentiality and trustworthiness.

Action Steps:
- Dedicate time to explore and experiment with various fear management apps to find the most suitable ones.
- Identify apps that align with personal preferences, whether focusing on mindfulness, cognitive restructuring, or community support.
- Incorporate the selected apps into daily or weekly routines for consistent and ongoing support.
- Participate in forums or communities within these apps to connect with others experiencing similar fears.
- Stay informed about updates and new features in fear management apps to optimize their effectiveness over time.

2. Mindfulness Meditation Apps for Fear Reduction:
Overviews:
- Mindfulness meditation apps provide guided practices that can significantly contribute to reducing fear and stress.
- These apps typically offer a variety of meditation sessions, allowing users to choose based on duration, focus, and personal preferences.
- Mindfulness meditation fosters present-moment awareness, which can be particularly effective in managing fear and anxiety.
- Incorporating technology into mindfulness practices enhances accessibility and encourages regular engagement.

Explorations:
- Explore popular mindfulness meditation apps such as Headspace, Calm, or Insight Timer.
- Examine the range of meditation sessions offered, including those specifically designed for fear, anxiety, or stress reduction.
- Experiment with different meditation styles, such as guided, unguided, or themed sessions, to identify what resonates best.
- Understand the additional features within these apps, such as sleep aids, breathing exercises, or daily mindfulness challenges.
- Investigate any scientific or evidence-based foundations behind the mindfulness practices incorporated in these apps.

Action Steps:

- Download a mindfulness meditation app and customize settings to align with personal preferences.
- Establish a daily meditation routine, starting with shorter sessions and gradually extending the duration.
- Experiment with different mindfulness practices within the app to find the most effective ones for fear reduction.
- Utilize features that track progress and provide insights into the consistency and impact of mindfulness practices.
- Integrate mindfulness meditation into daily life, incorporating sessions during breaks, stressful moments, or before bedtime.

3. Cognitive-Behavioral Therapy (CBT) Apps for Fear Challenges:

Overviews:

- Cognitive-Behavioral Therapy (CBT) apps leverage evidence-based techniques to address and modify thought patterns associated with fear.
- These apps often include interactive features, such as journaling, goal-setting, and cognitive restructuring exercises.
- CBT apps empower individuals to identify and challenge negative thought patterns, promoting more adaptive responses to fear.
- Incorporating technology into CBT allows for convenient and structured self-guided therapy.
- The goal-oriented nature of CBT apps provides a systematic approach to understanding and overcoming specific fear challenges.

Explorations:

- Explore CBT apps like Woebot, MoodKit, or What's Up? that are designed to address fear and anxiety.
- Examine the educational components within these apps, including psychoeducation on fear, anxiety cycles, and coping strategies.
- Experiment with the interactive features, such as mood tracking, thought records, and goal-setting exercises.
- Understand how these apps incorporate principles of exposure therapy to gradually confront and desensitize fear triggers.
- Investigate user reviews and expert endorsements to gauge the credibility and effectiveness of the CBT apps.

Action Steps:

- Choose a CBT app that aligns with personal goals and the specific nature of fear challenges.
- Invest time in understanding the educational content provided within the app to build a foundation for overcoming fear.
- Commit to regular use of the CBT app, integrating it into daily or weekly routines for ongoing support.
- Actively engage with interactive exercises, such as thought restructuring and goal-setting, to address fear triggers.
- Periodically assess progress using the tracking features, adjusting goals and strategies as needed.

4. Community Support Platforms for Shared Fear Experiences:

Overviews:

- Community support platforms leverage technology to connect individuals facing similar fear challenges, fostering a sense of shared experience.
- Online communities, forums, or social media groups dedicated to fear management provide a space for empathy, advice, and encouragement.
- The anonymity of online platforms can encourage open and honest sharing of experiences related to fear.
- Technology facilitates the formation of a global support network, transcending geographical boundaries.
- Community support platforms often include diverse perspectives, offering insights and coping strategies that individuals might not have considered.

Explorations:

- Explore online platforms such as Reddit communities, dedicated forums, or social media groups focused on fear and anxiety.

- Examine the types of discussions and topics commonly shared within these communities to understand the breadth of experiences.
- Evaluate the level of moderation and support within these platforms to ensure a safe and constructive environment.
- Participate in discussions, sharing personal experiences, challenges, and strategies for overcoming fear.
- Understand the potential benefits of forming connections and friendships within these online communities.

Action Steps:
- Find and join a community support platform that aligns with the specific nature of your fear.
- Actively participate in discussions, sharing experiences, insights, and supporting others in their fear management journey.
- Respect and utilize the anonymity provided by these platforms to share openly and honestly.
- Be aware of the level of moderation on the platform and report any inappropriate or harmful content.
- Consider forming offline connections with individuals from the online community for deeper support and understanding.

5. Educational Apps for Fear Understanding and Coping Strategies:

Overviews:
- Educational apps on fear provide information, resources, and coping strategies to enhance understanding and resilience.
- These apps often include modules on fear psychology, physiological responses, and evidence-based interventions.
- Incorporating gamification and interactive elements, educational apps make the learning process engaging and memorable.
- Users gain a comprehensive understanding of fear, enabling them to approach challenges with informed strategies.

Explorations:
- Explore educational apps like FearTools, Wysa, or Sanvello that focus on providing information and coping mechanisms for fear.
- Examine the structure of these apps, including the presence of modules, quizzes, and interactive content.
- Experiment with gamified elements that make the learning process enjoyable and facilitate better retention of information.
- Understand the integration of evidence-based interventions and therapeutic principles within these educational apps.

Action Steps:
- Choose an educational app that aligns with personal preferences and provides a comprehensive approach to understanding fear.
- Follow the structured modules and learning paths within the app to build a foundational understanding of fear.
- Actively participate in quizzes, activities, or interactive elements to reinforce learning.
- Apply the knowledge gained from the app to real-life situations, practicing coping strategies and interventions.

Chapter **26**

Support Systems:
The Role of Friends and Family

1. Overview of Support Systems:
Overviews:
- Support systems, comprising friends and family, play a pivotal role in fostering emotional well-being and resilience.
- These networks provide a foundation of trust, understanding, and empathy crucial for managing and overcoming fear.
- Friends and family serve as valuable sounding boards, offering diverse perspectives and insights.
- Emotional support from loved ones contributes to a sense of security, reducing the impact of fear-inducing situations.
- Building and maintaining strong support systems is an ongoing and reciprocal process that enhances overall mental health.

Explorations:
- Explore the dynamics of your existing support system, identifying key individuals and understanding the nature of your relationships.
- Reflect on past instances where support from friends and family positively influenced your ability to cope with fear.
- Consider cultural and individual differences in how support is expressed and received within your social circles.
- Explore the concept of reciprocal support, understanding how you contribute to the well-being of your friends and family.
- Examine the role of communication in support systems, focusing on effective expression of needs and active listening.

Action Steps:
- Reflect on the current state of your support system, identifying strengths and areas for improvement.
- Practice open communication with friends and family, expressing your needs and fears when appropriate.
- Develop active listening skills to better understand the concerns and fears of your loved ones.
- Dedicate quality time to nurture relationships, fostering a deeper connection with friends and family.
- Actively seek opportunities to support others in your network, creating a reciprocal and mutually beneficial dynamic.

2. The Impact of Social Connection on Fear Management:
Overviews:
- Social connection is a fundamental human need that significantly influences emotional well-being and fear management.
- Strong social ties contribute to a sense of belonging, reducing feelings of isolation and fear.
- The neurobiological impact of social connection includes the release of oxytocin, a hormone associated with trust and bonding.
- The fear of judgment is often mitigated within supportive social circles, promoting authenticity and vulnerability.
- Positive social interactions act as a buffer against the physiological and psychological effects of fear.

Explorations:
- Explore the role of social connection in your life, considering both in-person and virtual interactions.
- Reflect on how a sense of belonging within a community or social group influences your overall well-being.
- Investigate the physiological aspects of social connection, understanding how oxytocin release impacts fear response.
- Examine the influence of social dynamics on your comfort level in expressing fears and vulnerabilities.

- Consider the balance between social engagement and personal boundaries, exploring what feels most supportive for you.

Action Steps:
- Assess the quality and diversity of your social connections, identifying areas for expansion or strengthening.
- Explore joining clubs, groups, or online communities that align with your interests to foster new connections.
- Practice expressing vulnerability within your trusted social circles, gradually sharing fears and concerns.
- Be mindful of the impact of social interactions on your mood and fear levels, adjusting as needed.
- Establish healthy boundaries in social interactions, ensuring a balance between connection and personal space.

3. Building and Nurturing Healthy Relationships:

Overviews:
- Healthy relationships contribute to emotional resilience by providing a secure and supportive foundation.
- Trust, effective communication, and mutual respect are pillars of healthy relationships that counteract fear.
- Unhealthy relationship dynamics can amplify fear and stress, underscoring the importance of evaluating and addressing them.
- Nurturing positive relationships involves continuous effort, understanding, and adaptation to changing circumstances.
- Building a diverse network of relationships, including friendships, family, and romantic connections, enhances overall support.

Explorations:
- Reflect on the qualities of your existing relationships, identifying strengths and areas for improvement.
- Explore the impact of healthy relationship dynamics on your overall emotional well-being and fear resilience.
- Identify and address any patterns of unhealthy communication or power imbalances within your relationships.
- Consider the role of empathy in fostering understanding and emotional support within relationships.
- Explore the concept of relational self-awareness, understanding how your fears and experiences intersect with those of your loved ones.

Action Steps:
- Reflect on the current state of your relationships, acknowledging positive aspects and areas for growth.
- Practice open and effective communication within your relationships, fostering understanding and trust.
- Develop skills for constructive conflict resolution, addressing challenges openly and collaboratively.
- Dedicate quality time to strengthen connections, engaging in activities that foster shared experiences.
- Cultivate a diverse network of relationships, recognizing the unique support each connection can provide.

4. Recognizing and Addressing Toxic Relationships:

Overviews:
- Toxic relationships can significantly contribute to fear and emotional distress, impacting mental health.
- Recognizing signs of toxicity, such as manipulation or constant negativity, is crucial for preserving well-being.
- The fear of ending toxic relationships may be a barrier, emphasizing the importance of setting boundaries for self-preservation.
- Addressing toxic dynamics involves prioritizing self-care and seeking professional support when necessary.
- Creating distance or ending toxic relationships is a courageous step toward fostering a fear-resilient and healthy emotional environment.

Explorations:

- Reflect on your relationships to identify any patterns of toxicity, considering emotional, psychological, or verbal abuse.
- Explore the emotional toll of toxic relationships on your overall well-being and fear response.
- Investigate the reasons for hesitation in addressing toxic dynamics, acknowledging any fears or barriers.
- Examine the impact of setting and enforcing boundaries on your ability to manage fear within relationships.
- Consider seeking support from friends, family, or professionals when navigating the challenges of toxic relationships.

Action Steps:

- Educate yourself on signs of toxic relationships, objectively evaluating your own connections.
- Identify and communicate clear boundaries within toxic relationships, prioritizing your well-being.
- Reflect on any internal fears or beliefs that may be contributing to the reluctance to address toxicity.
- Reach out to trusted friends, family, or mental health professionals for guidance and support.
- If necessary, take gradual steps to create distance or end toxic relationships, prioritizing your mental and emotional health.

5. Collective Support: The Strength of Family Bonds:

Overviews:

- Family bonds offer a unique and foundational form of support, influencing emotional resilience.
- The collective strength of a united family provides a powerful source of comfort and security in the face of fear.
- Shared values, traditions, and experiences within a family contribute to a sense of identity and belonging.
- The intergenerational aspect of family bonds can offer wisdom, guidance, and diverse perspectives on managing fear.

Explorations:

- Reflect on the role of your family in shaping your beliefs, values, and responses to fear.
- Explore the cultural and generational aspects of your family's approach to fear management.
- Investigate how shared experiences within the family contribute to a sense of unity and support.
- Consider the impact of chosen family members or close friends who serve as additional pillars of support.
- Examine the role of communication and transparency within the family unit in addressing and managing collective fears.

Action Steps:

- Strengthen connections within your family through open communication and shared activities.
- Initiate conversations with older family members to gain insights into their experiences with fear.
- Acknowledge and express gratitude for chosen family members or close friends who provide additional support.
- Explore and celebrate the cultural aspects of your family that contribute to a unique support system.
- Encourage collaborative approaches to fear management within the family, fostering a sense of unity and resilience.

Chapter 27

Finding the Right Therapist:
Professional Help for Fear

1. Overview of Finding the Right Therapist:
Overviews:
- Seeking the right therapist is a crucial step in addressing and managing fear, providing professional guidance and support.
- Therapists offer specialized skills and tools to help individuals navigate the complexities of fear and related emotions.
- The therapeutic relationship serves as a safe and confidential space for exploring fears, traumas, and personal growth.
- Finding the right therapist involves considering various factors, including therapeutic approaches, specialties, and personal compatibility.
- The therapeutic process is a collaborative journey where individuals actively participate in their own healing and self-discovery.

Explorations:
- Explore your motivations for seeking therapy, identifying specific fears, challenges, or goals you want to address.
- Reflect on your preferred therapeutic approach, considering options such as cognitive-behavioral therapy, psychodynamic therapy, or mindfulness-based therapy.
- Investigate therapists' specialties and expertise, aligning them with your specific areas of concern or interest.
- Explore different therapy formats, including individual, group, or online therapy, to find the most suitable setting for your needs.

Action Steps:
- Clearly define your therapy goals, whether they involve fear management, personal growth, or specific behavioral changes.
- Learn about different therapeutic approaches and identify the ones that resonate with your preferences and needs.
- Seek therapists with expertise in areas relevant to your concerns, ensuring a tailored and effective therapeutic experience.
- Explore different therapy formats, attending initial sessions or consultations to gauge comfort and effectiveness.

2. Building Trust and Rapport in Therapy:
Overviews:
- Building trust and rapport with a therapist is foundational for a successful therapeutic journey in fear management.
- Trust allows individuals to share openly, explore vulnerabilities, and engage in the therapeutic process authentically.
- Rapport facilitates effective communication, ensuring a collaborative and supportive therapeutic relationship.
- Establishing trust is an ongoing process that involves open communication, consistency, and mutual respect.
- A strong therapeutic alliance enhances the effectiveness of therapeutic interventions and promotes a sense of safety.

Explorations:
- Reflect on past experiences in therapy, identifying factors that contributed to or hindered the development of trust.
- Explore your comfort level in expressing vulnerability and discussing fears, considering factors that may impact openness.

- Investigate the therapist's approach to building trust, examining their communication style, empathy, and commitment to confidentiality.
- Understand the importance of mutual respect in the therapeutic relationship, exploring how it contributes to a positive therapeutic alliance.

Action Steps:
- Reflect on personal experiences related to trust in relationships, identifying patterns and preferences.
- Communicate openly with your therapist about your expectations, fears, and any concerns related to the therapeutic process.
- Provide feedback to your therapist about the effectiveness of their approach and any adjustments needed to enhance trust.

3. Tailoring Therapeutic Approaches to Fear:
Overviews:
- Fear is a complex emotion that may require tailored therapeutic approaches to address its unique manifestations.
- Therapists employ a variety of techniques, such as exposure therapy, cognitive restructuring, or mindfulness, depending on individual needs.
- Tailoring therapeutic interventions involves a collaborative process between the therapist and the individual, considering preferences and comfort levels.
- Different therapeutic modalities, including traditional talk therapy, art therapy, or somatic experiencing, offer diverse tools for fear management.
- The flexibility to adapt therapeutic approaches ensures a personalized and effective treatment plan for fear-related concerns.

Explorations:
- Explore your own preferences and comfort levels with various therapeutic modalities, considering past experiences or inclinations.
- Reflect on the specific manifestations of fear in your life, identifying triggers, thought patterns, and behavioral responses.
- Investigate therapeutic approaches commonly used for fear management, understanding their principles and potential benefits.
- Discuss with your therapist the flexibility to explore different techniques and modalities, ensuring a personalized and adaptable treatment plan.

Action Steps:
- Communicate your preferences and comfort levels with therapeutic approaches, ensuring alignment with your goals.
- Collaborate with your therapist to identify specific triggers, cognitive patterns, and behavioral responses related to fear.
- Engage in discussions with your therapist about the various therapeutic approaches available for fear management.
- Express the desire for flexibility in exploring and adapting therapeutic techniques based on your evolving needs.
- Consider integrating holistic approaches into therapy, incorporating mindfulness, lifestyle adjustments, and complementary practices.

4. Navigating Fear Traumas:
Overviews:
- Fear traumas, such as phobias or post-traumatic stress, require specialized therapeutic approaches for effective resolution.
- Therapists use evidence-based interventions, including EMDR, exposure therapy, or trauma-focused cognitive-behavioral therapy, to address fear-related traumas.
- Understanding the impact of fear traumas on daily functioning and mental well-being is crucial for developing a targeted treatment plan.
- Therapists create a safe space for individuals to explore and process fear traumas, fostering healing and resilience.

Explorations:
- Explore any fear traumas in your life, recognizing their impact on your emotional and psychological well-being.

- Reflect on the specific symptoms or challenges associated with fear traumas, considering how they manifest in different situations.
- Investigate therapeutic modalities designed for trauma resolution, understanding their principles and potential benefits.
- Examine your readiness and comfort level in addressing fear traumas in therapy, acknowledging any concerns or hesitations.

Action Steps:
- Acknowledge and recognize fear traumas, understanding their impact on daily life and emotional well-being.
- Collaborate with your therapist to identify specific symptoms or challenges related to fear traumas.
- Discuss with your therapist the available therapeutic modalities for trauma resolution, exploring their suitability for your needs.
- Reflect on your readiness to address fear traumas in therapy, openly communicating any concerns with your therapist.
- Prioritize the establishment of safety and support within the therapeutic relationship, recognizing their crucial role in navigating fear traumas.

5. Long-Term Strategies for Fear Maintenance:
Overviews:
- Long-term fear maintenance involves developing strategies and skills that extend beyond the therapeutic setting.
- Therapists collaborate with individuals to build a toolbox of coping mechanisms, resilience skills, and ongoing self-awareness practices.
- Recognizing the cyclical nature of fear, long-term strategies aim to empower individuals to navigate future challenges with confidence.
- Self-monitoring and regular check-ins with a therapist contribute to the sustainability of fear management strategies over time.

Explorations:
- Explore the concept of long-term fear maintenance, understanding its significance in sustaining mental and emotional well-being.
- Reflect on past experiences of implementing coping mechanisms or resilience strategies and their effectiveness in fear management.
- Investigate self-awareness practices that contribute to ongoing emotional regulation and mindfulness in daily life.
- Examine the role of self-monitoring in recognizing early signs of fear escalation and proactively implementing coping strategies.

Action Steps:
- Engage in discussions with your therapist about the concept and importance of long-term fear maintenance.
- Reflect on past experiences with coping mechanisms, identifying strategies that have proven effective in fear management.
- Explore and incorporate self-awareness practices into daily life, such as mindfulness, journaling, or reflective exercises.
- Collaborate with your therapist to create a self-monitoring plan, identifying early signs of fear escalation and appropriate interventions.

Chapter 28

Ethical Considerations:
When Fear Protects Us

1. Understanding Ethical Considerations:
Overviews:

- Ethical considerations in fear management involve navigating situations where fear serves as a protective mechanism.
- Balancing ethical principles requires careful examination of the potential harm or benefit associated with fear-driven actions.
- Fear can prompt ethical dilemmas, requiring individuals to evaluate the consequences of their choices on themselves and others.
- Ethical considerations extend to how fear influences decision-making, relationships, and the broader societal context.
- Recognizing the dual nature of fear, as both a safeguard and a potential source of bias, is crucial for ethical decision-making.

Explorations:

- Reflect on personal experiences where fear played a role in decision-making and ethical considerations.
- Explore cultural, societal, and contextual influences on the ethical dimensions of fear-driven actions.
- Examine case studies or scenarios where fear protectionism may clash with ethical principles.
- Investigate the psychological mechanisms behind fear-induced ethical dilemmas and decision biases.
- Understand the interplay between fear, empathy, and ethical considerations in interpersonal relationships.

Action Steps:

- Engage in regular reflection on fear-driven decisions, considering their ethical implications.
- Develop cultural sensitivity by exploring how fear and ethics are intertwined in different cultural contexts.
- Analyze case studies or real-life scenarios involving fear and ethical considerations.
- Enhance psychological awareness of fear-induced biases, fostering mindful decision-making.
- Cultivate empathy to better understand the ethical dimensions of fear in relationships and societal contexts.

2. Fear as a Moral Compass:
Overviews:

- Fear can act as a moral compass, signaling situations that challenge personal values or ethical principles.
- Recognizing fear as a moral guide involves discerning whether the fear response aligns with one's core values.
- Ethical decision-making considers the alignment of fear with universally accepted moral principles.
- Understanding the nuances of fear-driven morality requires introspection and a deep exploration of personal values.
- Balancing fear as a protective mechanism with ethical decision-making involves refining one's moral compass.

Explorations:

- Reflect on instances where fear prompted a moral dilemma or raised ethical questions.
- Explore how personal values and ethical frameworks influence the interpretation of fear signals.
- Examine the intersection of fear, morality, and decision-making in various life domains.
- Investigate philosophical perspectives on fear-driven morality and its implications.
- Understand the role of empathy and compassion in fear-driven ethical considerations.

Action Steps:

- Clarify personal values through introspection and self-discovery.
- Analyze past scenarios where fear acted as a moral compass, dissecting the ethical dimensions.

- Explore interdisciplinary perspectives, including philosophy and psychology, on fear and morality.
- Engage in philosophical inquiry regarding fear's role in shaping ethical decisions.
- Actively work on developing empathy as a tool for understanding and navigating fear-driven moral dilemmas.

3. Ethical Decision-Making in Fearful Situations:
Overviews:
- Ethical decision-making in fearful situations involves a deliberate and conscientious approach to choices.
- Balancing the need for self-protection with ethical principles requires a nuanced understanding of the situation.
- Fear-driven decisions can be ethically sound when aligned with principles such as justice, beneficence, and autonomy.
- The ethical dimensions of fear extend beyond individual actions to include considerations for broader social impact.
- Developing ethical decision-making skills in fear-inducing scenarios enhances personal and societal well-being.

Explorations:
- Reflect on personal experiences where ethical decision-making was influenced by fear.
- Explore ethical theories and frameworks that provide guidance in fear-driven decision-making.
- Examine the impact of fear on empathy, compassion, and consideration for others in decision-making.
- Investigate real-world examples where ethical considerations played a pivotal role in fear-induced choices.
- Understand the intersectionality of fear, ethics, and power dynamics in social and organizational contexts.

Action Steps:
- Engage in reflective practices, analyzing cases where fear influenced ethical decisions.
- Familiarize yourself with ethical theories and frameworks applicable to fear management.
- Cultivate empathy as a guiding force in fear-driven ethical decision-making.
- Consider the broader societal impact of fear-driven decisions to ensure ethical responsibility.
- Attend workshops or engage in activities focused on ethical decision-making, specifically in fear-inducing situations.

4. Navigating Ethical Grey Areas in Fear:
Overviews:
- Fear often introduces ethical grey areas, where the right course of action may be unclear or contested.
- Recognizing and navigating these grey areas require a commitment to ethical principles and ongoing self-reflection.
- Ethical ambiguity in fear situations underscores the complexity of balancing personal safety and moral responsibility.
- The subjective nature of fear-induced ethical challenges necessitates open dialogue and a diversity of perspectives.
- Engaging with ambiguity in fear-driven decisions provides opportunities for ethical growth and resilience.

Explorations:
- Reflect on experiences where fear created ethical grey areas, challenging traditional notions of right and wrong.
- Explore the cultural, societal, and individual factors that contribute to the perception of ethical ambiguity in fear.
- Examine the role of communication and transparency in navigating ethical grey areas related to fear.
- Investigate case studies or historical examples where fear-induced decisions faced ethical scrutiny.
- Understand the ethical implications of power dynamics and privilege in navigating fear-driven grey areas.

Action Steps:
- Engage in regular self-reflection to identify personal biases and perceptions of ethical grey areas.
- Seek diverse perspectives and engage in open conversations about fear-induced ethical challenges.
- Analyze cases where fear created ethical ambiguity, dissecting the factors at play.

- Enhance communication skills to navigate and discuss ethical grey areas effectively.
- Participate in training programs that focus on developing ethical resilience in fear-related decision-making.

5. Beyond Self: Ethical Considerations in Fearful Leadership:

Overviews:
- Ethical leadership in fear involves a responsibility to consider not only personal well-being but also the impact on others.
- Fearful leaders must balance the ethical dimensions of decision-making with the welfare of their teams and stakeholders.
- The influence of fear on leadership style requires a commitment to transparency, integrity, and ethical principles.
- Ethical considerations in leadership extend to fostering a culture of psychological safety and well-being.
- Fear-aware leaders actively engage in ongoing ethical self-assessment and seek feedback to improve decision-making.

Explorations:
- Reflect on experiences where fear influenced leadership decisions and explore the ethical dimensions of those choices.
- Examine how fear in leadership intersects with organizational culture, values, and long-term goals.
- Explore leadership models that integrate ethical considerations in fear management within organizational settings.
- Investigate the role of empathy and emotional intelligence in ethical leadership during fear-inducing situations.

Action Steps:
- Regularly assess personal leadership decisions in fear-inducing situations from an ethical standpoint.
- Ensure alignment between organizational values and fear-driven leadership decisions.
- Engage in continuous learning about ethical leadership and its application in fear management.
- Seek feedback from team members regarding the ethical dimensions of leadership decisions during fear-inducing moments.
- Develop ethical crisis response plans that prioritize well-being and transparency in fear-inducing situations.

Chapter 29

Retraining the Brain:
Neuroplasticity and Fear

1. Neuroplasticity Fundamentals:
Overviews:
- Neuroplasticity is the brain's ability to reorganize and adapt by forming new neural connections.
- Understanding neuroplasticity provides insights into the brain's capacity for change, even in the context of fear.
- The brain's plasticity is influenced by experiences, environment, and intentional mental exercises.
- Neuroplasticity plays a pivotal role in shaping responses to fear and reprogramming habitual thought patterns.
- Leveraging neuroplasticity involves engaging in targeted practices to foster positive brain rewiring.

Explorations:
- Explore scientific literature on the mechanisms and principles of neuroplasticity.
- Examine case studies showcasing how neuroplasticity contributes to overcoming fear-related challenges.
- Investigate the impact of various external factors, such as stress and lifestyle, on neuroplasticity.
- Understand the role of neuroplasticity in both short-term fear responses and long-term behavioral changes.
- Explore the intersection of neuroplasticity with emotional regulation and fear resilience.

Action Steps:
- Engage with books, articles, or courses on neuroplasticity to deepen understanding.
- Integrate mindfulness meditation into daily routines to enhance neuroplasticity.
- Consider neurofeedback sessions to directly train the brain for specific fear responses.
- Participate in CBT, a therapeutic approach leveraging neuroplasticity for fear reduction.
- Explore brain-training apps or games designed to stimulate neuroplastic changes.

2. Rewiring Fear Responses:
Overviews:
- Rewiring fear responses involves altering neural pathways associated with fear triggers.
- Intentional efforts can shift the brain from automatic fear reactions to more measured and controlled responses.
- Fear responses are malleable, and targeted interventions can foster adaptive reactions.
- Consistent practice is key to solidifying new neural patterns that support healthier responses to fear.
- Rewiring fear responses contributes to increased emotional regulation and a sense of empowerment.

Explorations:
- Explore research on interventions proven to rewire neural pathways related to fear.
- Investigate the role of emotional memory in the formation and modification of fear-related neural circuits.
- Examine how neuroplasticity is harnessed in therapeutic settings to address specific phobias or traumas.
- Understand the connection between mindfulness-based practices and the rewiring of fear responses.
- Explore personal narratives or testimonials of individuals who successfully rewired their fear responses.

Action Steps:
- Engage in exposure therapy under the guidance of a mental health professional to recondition fear responses.
- Gradually expose yourself to fear triggers, allowing the brain to adapt incrementally.
- Incorporate mind-body practices like yoga or tai chi to promote holistic neural changes.
- Integrate positive affirmations to reshape thought patterns associated with fear.

- Maintain a fear journal to track progress, setbacks, and evolving emotional responses.

3. Cognitive Restructuring:

Overviews:

- Cognitive restructuring involves challenging and modifying irrational or distorted thought patterns.
- The process is rooted in neuroplasticity, aiming to create new, balanced perspectives on fear-inducing stimuli.
- Cognitive restructuring enhances the brain's flexibility in interpreting and responding to fear cues.
- Integrating this approach contributes to more adaptive behaviors and emotional states.
- Consistent cognitive restructuring can lead to lasting changes in neural networks associated with fear.

Explorations:

- Explore the theoretical foundations of cognitive restructuring within the framework of neuroplasticity.
- Investigate how cognitive restructuring is applied in therapeutic modalities such as Cognitive Behavioral Therapy (CBT).
- Examine the role of self-awareness in identifying and challenging distorted thought patterns linked to fear.
- Understand the connection between cognitive restructuring and the brain's capacity to create new synaptic connections.

Action Steps:

- Engage in regular self-reflection to identify automatic negative thoughts related to fear.
- Seek CBT sessions with a qualified therapist to learn and apply cognitive restructuring techniques.
- Practice mindfulness to cultivate awareness of thought patterns and initiate cognitive shifts.
- Keep a thought journal to record and challenge fear-related thoughts systematically.
- Incorporate positive visualization techniques to reframe perceptions of fear-inducing situations.

4. Building Neuroplasticity through Learning:

Overviews:

- Learning new skills and acquiring knowledge contribute to the ongoing process of neuroplasticity.
- The brain's adaptability extends to acquiring expertise and refining abilities related to fear management.
- Lifelong learning promotes cognitive health, resilience, and a more nuanced understanding of fear.
- The intersection of learning and neuroplasticity highlights the brain's capacity for growth and development.
- Actively engaging in diverse learning experiences can counteract stagnation and contribute to fearless living.

Explorations:

- Explore the neuroscience of learning and its impact on neural plasticity, particularly in the context of fear.
- Investigate how acquiring new skills or knowledge domains can influence fear responses.
- Examine the role of curiosity and exploration in fostering neuroplastic changes associated with fear.
- Understand the concept of cognitive reserve and how continual learning contributes to overall brain health.
- Explore the experiences of individuals who embraced lifelong learning as a strategy for fear management.

Action Steps:

- Identify a skill or area of knowledge you want to develop and commit to regular practice.
- Enroll in courses, workshops, or pursue self-directed learning in areas of personal interest.
- Seek out learning experiences that challenge existing comfort zones, fostering adaptability.
- Embrace interdisciplinary learning to stimulate diverse areas of the brain.
- Share your knowledge or skills with others, reinforcing learning through teaching.

5. Mindful Awareness and Neuroplasticity:

Overviews:

- Mindful awareness practices contribute to neuroplastic changes by enhancing attention and focus.
- The intentional focus on the present moment in mindfulness positively influences brain structure and function.
- Mindfulness promotes emotional regulation, reducing the impact of fear on neural pathways.

- Cultivating mindful awareness involves non-judgmental observation, a key aspect of neuroplasticity.
- Regular mindfulness practice contributes to an overall sense of well-being and fear resilience.

Explorations:
- Explore scientific studies on the relationship between mindfulness, brain plasticity, and fear reduction.
- Investigate different mindfulness techniques and their specific effects on neural structures associated with fear.
- Examine the role of mindful awareness in breaking habitual fear responses and promoting adaptability.
- Understand the connection between mindfulness and the brain's default mode network in fear processing.
- Explore how mindfulness contributes to changes in neural connectivity related to attention and emotional regulation.

Action Steps:
- Establish a daily mindfulness routine, incorporating techniques like meditation or mindful breathing.
- Practice mindful eating to bring awareness to the sensory experience of food and break automatic stress responses.
- Engage in body scan meditations to enhance awareness of physical sensations and emotional states.
- Integrate mindful movement practices such as yoga or tai chi into your routine.
- Consider participating in mindfulness retreats for immersive and focused mindfulness experiences.

Chapter **30**

The Bravery of Boundaries:
Saying No Without Guilt

1. Establishing the Importance of Boundaries:
Overviews:
- Setting boundaries is an essential aspect of self-care and maintaining emotional well-being.
- Healthy boundaries create a framework for positive relationships and personal growth.
- The ability to say no without guilt is rooted in a clear understanding of one's needs and limitations.
- Boundaries contribute to a sense of empowerment, fostering resilience in the face of external pressures.
- Recognizing that establishing and communicating boundaries is an ongoing process crucial for personal development.

Explorations:
- Explore psychological theories on the role of boundaries in fostering psychological health.
- Examine the impact of boundary violations on mental and emotional well-being.
- Investigate cultural and societal influences on the perception and acceptance of personal boundaries.
- Understand the connection between assertiveness, self-esteem, and the establishment of healthy boundaries.
- Explore case studies showcasing the transformative effects of implementing and maintaining boundaries.

Action Steps:
- Engage in reflective practices to identify areas where personal boundaries may need reinforcement.
- Attend workshops or seminars focused on learning effective boundary-setting strategies.
- Keep a boundary journal to track instances where setting boundaries led to positive outcomes.
- Enhance assertiveness and communication skills to express boundaries clearly.
- Use visualization techniques to imagine positive scenarios where boundaries are respected and honored.

2. Overcoming Guilt Associated with Saying No:
Overviews:
- Guilt often accompanies the act of saying no, stemming from societal expectations or fear of disappointing others.
- Understanding that setting boundaries is a self-affirming act can help mitigate guilt.
- Recognizing the distinction between healthy self-care and selfishness is key to overcoming guilt.
- Cultivating self-compassion and acknowledging the right to prioritize personal needs contributes to guilt reduction.
- Learning to reframe guilt as a signal for potential boundary violations rather than an inherent flaw.

Explorations:
- Explore psychological research on the emotions of guilt and its impact on decision-making.
- Examine cultural norms and their influence on guilt associated with prioritizing personal boundaries.
- Understand the connection between guilt and the fear of rejection or social disapproval.
- Investigate therapeutic approaches to address guilt, such as cognitive restructuring or mindfulness-based interventions.
- Explore narratives of individuals who successfully navigated guilt while establishing and maintaining boundaries.

Action Steps:
- Maintain a guilt journal to identify patterns and triggers associated with saying no.
- Integrate self-compassion exercises to counteract guilt with kindness toward oneself.
- Develop daily affirmation rituals to reinforce the positive aspects of setting and maintaining boundaries.
- Seek therapy or counseling to explore and address the root causes of guilt in boundary-setting.

3. Assertive Communication in Boundary Setting:

Overviews:

- Assertive communication is a cornerstone in effectively expressing and upholding personal boundaries.
- The ability to articulate needs and limits with clarity and respect is central to successful boundary setting.
- Developing assertiveness involves balancing openness with the firmness required to maintain boundaries.
- Assertive communication fosters mutual understanding and reduces the likelihood of misunderstandings or conflicts.
- Recognizing that assertiveness is a skill that can be cultivated and refined over time.

Explorations:

- Explore psychological frameworks on assertive communication and its impact on interpersonal relationships.
- Examine the role of body language and non-verbal cues in conveying assertiveness and boundary setting.
- Understand the psychological benefits of assertiveness for both the individual setting boundaries and those receiving the message.
- Investigate cultural variations in the perception and acceptance of assertive communication and boundary setting.
- Explore case studies illustrating the positive outcomes of assertive communication in various contexts.

Action Steps:

- Engage in role-playing exercises to practice assertive communication in different situations.
- Attend workshops focused on developing assertive communication skills.
- Seek feedback and support from friends or peers when practicing assertive communication.
- Integrate mindfulness practices to enhance awareness and presence in communication.
- Maintain a journal to reflect on assertive communication experiences, noting challenges and successes.

4. Navigating Resistance and Responses:

Overviews:

- Setting boundaries may be met with various responses, including resistance, negotiation, or acceptance.
- Anticipating potential reactions allows for proactive and thoughtful navigation of boundary-setting scenarios.
- The fear of negative responses can be a barrier to boundary setting, emphasizing the importance of resilience.
- Recognizing that others' reactions are not always within one's control is crucial in maintaining self-efficacy.
- Learning to navigate resistance with poise and persistence contributes to the effectiveness of boundary setting.

Explorations:

- Explore psychological theories on interpersonal resistance and negotiation in the context of boundaries.
- Examine case studies highlighting successful strategies for navigating resistance to personal boundaries.
- Understand the role of empathy in anticipating and responding to others' reactions to boundary setting.
- Investigate cultural and contextual factors influencing diverse responses to boundary establishment.
- Explore narratives of individuals who faced resistance but successfully maintained their boundaries.

Action Steps:

- Anticipate potential scenarios and responses to boundary setting, preparing effective responses.
- Establish a support network to turn to for guidance and encouragement during challenging situations.
- Integrate resilience-building activities, such as mindfulness or self-reflection, into daily routines.
- Develop negotiation skills to navigate compromises without compromising essential boundaries.
- After boundary-setting encounters, reflect on the experience to gather insights for continuous improvement.

5. Sustainable Boundary Maintenance:

Overviews:

- Sustainable boundary maintenance involves the ongoing reinforcement and adaptation of personal limits.
- Recognizing that boundaries may need adjustment based on evolving circumstances is essential for longevity.
- Sustainable boundaries contribute to long-term emotional well-being, reducing the likelihood of burnout or resentment.
- Consistent communication and reinforcement of boundaries solidify their presence in relationships and personal dynamics.
- The ability to sustain boundaries over time is a testament to one's commitment to self-care and fearless living.

Explorations:

- Explore theories on the long-term impact of sustainable boundary maintenance on mental health.
- Examine cultural attitudes toward persistent boundary-setting and its acceptance over time.
- Understand the role of adaptability in sustaining boundaries amidst life changes and challenges.
- Investigate the connection between sustainable boundary setting and overall life satisfaction.
- Explore case studies of individuals who successfully maintained boundaries over extended periods.

Action Steps:

- Set aside dedicated time for regular reflection on the effectiveness and relevance of existing boundaries.
- Foster open communication in relationships to address evolving needs and expectations.
- Integrate ongoing self-care practices into daily routines to reinforce the importance of personal well-being.
- Develop rituals or practices to symbolize the ongoing commitment to maintaining boundaries.
- Seek guidance from mental health professionals or counselors for periodic boundary check-ins and adjustments.

Chapter **31**

Harnessing Hope:
Positivity as Fear's Counterbalance

1. Recognizing the Power of Hope:
Overviews:
- Hope serves as a potent force counterbalancing fear, providing a positive lens through which challenges can be approached.
- Understanding hope as an anticipatory emotion that envisions positive outcomes can transform one's mindset.
- Hope instills resilience by fostering a belief in one's capacity to navigate difficulties and uncertainties.
- The cultivation of hope involves acknowledging current challenges while maintaining a forward-looking perspective.
- Recognizing the symbiotic relationship between hope and courage, where each reinforces the other.

Explorations:
- Explore psychological theories on hope and its impact on mental health, particularly in the context of fear.
- Examine the role of hope in decision-making and problem-solving during challenging situations.
- Understand how cultural and societal narratives contribute to the promotion or hindrance of hope.
- Investigate the connection between hope and physiological well-being, such as reduced stress and improved immune function.
- Explore case studies showcasing individuals who harnessed hope to overcome significant fears.

Action Steps:
- Engage in daily or weekly journaling to reflect on hopeful thoughts, aspirations, and positive outcomes.
- Incorporate visualization techniques to imagine hopeful scenarios and successful fear confrontation.
- Cultivate a habit of expressing gratitude, focusing on positive aspects even amidst challenges.
- Create and recite affirmations that emphasize hope, resilience, and the ability to overcome fear.
- Read literature, stories, or quotes that inspire hope and optimism.

2. The Role of Positivity in Fear Resilience:
Overviews:
- Positivity, as a mindset, contributes significantly to fear resilience and overall mental well-being.
- A positive outlook involves reframing challenges, viewing them as opportunities for growth and learning.
- Positivity acts as a buffer against the detrimental effects of chronic stress and fear-related anxieties.
- The cultivation of a positive mindset is an ongoing practice that requires conscious effort and self-awareness.
- Recognizing the impact of positivity on interpersonal relationships, creating a ripple effect of emotional well-being.

Explorations:
- Explore psychological research on the benefits of positive thinking in reducing fear and anxiety.
- Examine the connection between a positive mindset and the brain's neuroplasticity, influencing fear response.
- Understand the cultural variations in the promotion of positivity and its impact on fear resilience.
- Investigate the correlation between positive emotions and increased psychological and physical resilience.
- Explore narratives of individuals who adopted a positive mindset to overcome pervasive fears.

Action Steps:
- Set aside time daily for reflection on positive aspects, achievements, or moments of gratitude.
- Engage in a positivity challenge, actively seeking and acknowledging positive elements in daily life.
- Create a visual board with positive affirmations and visual representations of hopeful outcomes.

- Incorporate mindfulness exercises to stay present and appreciate positive aspects of the current moment.
- Surround yourself with individuals who exude positivity, creating a supportive environment.

3. Cultivating Optimism in the Face of Fear:

Overviews:
- Optimism, characterized by a hopeful and positive outlook on the future, is a key component in fear resilience.
- Optimistic individuals tend to interpret challenges as temporary and surmountable, enhancing their ability to confront fear.
- Cultivating optimism involves challenging negative thought patterns and fostering a mindset of growth and possibility.
- Optimism contributes to increased motivation, adaptability, and an overall sense of well-being.
- Recognizing the distinction between realistic optimism and blind positivity is crucial for balanced fear resilience.

Explorations:
- Explore psychological theories on optimism and its influence on mental and emotional health.
- Examine the connection between optimistic thinking and the body's stress response, particularly in fear-inducing situations.
- Understand the impact of family and societal influences on the development of optimistic or pessimistic outlooks.
- Investigate the relationship between optimism and increased problem-solving abilities during fear-related challenges.
- Explore narratives of individuals who adopted an optimistic mindset to navigate and overcome persistent fears.

Action Steps:
- Document and challenge negative thoughts, replacing them with optimistic alternatives.
- Practice mindfulness techniques to stay present and cultivate an optimistic perspective.
- Engage in workshops or activities designed to enhance optimistic thinking and reframing.
- Set realistic yet optimistic goals, emphasizing growth and learning in the face of fear.
- Share optimism goals with a friend or partner, creating mutual support in cultivating positive outlooks.

4. Positivity as a Catalyst for Fear Action:

Overviews:
- Positivity serves as a catalyst for taking proactive steps in confronting and overcoming fear.
- A positive mindset enhances motivation, encouraging individuals to face challenges with a can-do attitude.
- Positivity acts as a counterbalance to fear-induced paralysis, promoting a sense of agency and empowerment.
- The connection between positive emotions and increased risk-taking behavior contributes to fear resilience.
- Recognizing the link between positivity and self-efficacy, fostering a belief in one's ability to influence outcomes.

Explorations:
- Explore psychological research on the relationship between positive emotions and risk-taking behavior.
- Examine case studies highlighting instances where positivity acted as a catalyst for fear action and confrontation.
- Understand how positive thinking influences the perception of challenges, turning them into opportunities.
- Investigate the impact of positive emotions on the body's physiological response to fear-inducing stimuli.
- Explore narratives of individuals who, fueled by positivity, took decisive actions to conquer their fears.

Action Steps:
- Develop a step-by-step plan for confronting specific fears, infused with positive affirmations.
- Identify and utilize positive anchors, such as objects or phrases, to evoke a positive mindset during fear-inducing situations.

- Use visualization techniques to imagine successful fear confrontation and the positive aftermath.
- Share fear action plans with a trusted friend or mentor, fostering accountability and encouragement.
- Acknowledge and celebrate each step taken in confronting fears, reinforcing positive behavior.

5. Building a Resilient Positivity Mindset:

Overviews:
- Building a resilient positivity mindset involves the intentional cultivation of positive thought patterns.
- Resilient positivity goes beyond fleeting moments of optimism, creating a sustained foundation for fear resilience.
- A resilient positivity mindset embraces setbacks as opportunities for growth, maintaining hope in challenging times.
- Consistent practice of positivity strengthens neural pathways associated with resilience and emotional well-being.
- Resilient positivity becomes a guiding force in decision-making, problem-solving, and overall life satisfaction.

Explorations:
- Explore the concept of resilience in positive psychology and its connection to sustained positivity.
- Examine the impact of resilient positivity on mental health, including reduced stress and improved emotional regulation.
- Understand how adversity and challenges contribute to the development of a resilient positivity mindset.
- Investigate the cultural variations in the promotion and acceptance of resilient positivity as a fear resilience strategy.
- Explore narratives of individuals who, through resilient positivity, navigated complex fears and emerged stronger.

Action Steps:
- Integrate a regular practice of reflecting on positive aspects amidst challenges.
- Develop rituals or habits that symbolize the commitment to maintaining a resilient positivity mindset.
- Engage in mindfulness activities that specifically focus on fostering a positive mental outlook.
- Maintain a journal documenting personal growth and positive transformations resulting from challenging experiences.
- Seek mentorship from individuals known for their resilient positivity, gaining insights and guidance.

Chapter 32

Fear and Culture:
Societal Impacts on Collective Anxiety

1. Cultural Foundations of Fear:
Overviews:
- Culture plays a foundational role in shaping collective fears, influencing societal norms, and individual perceptions.
- The interplay between cultural narratives, traditions, and historical events significantly contributes to the collective fears within a society.
- Examining cultural taboos and stigmas provides insights into the sources of anxiety deeply embedded in societal consciousness.
- Cultural values, religious beliefs, and socio-economic factors form a complex web that contributes to the manifestation of collective fears.
- Understanding the historical context of a culture unveils the roots of certain fears and anxieties prevalent within that community.

Explorations:
- Explore how cultural symbols and metaphors contribute to the creation and reinforcement of collective fears.
- Examine the impact of cultural narratives on the perception of specific threats, such as health crises, economic downturns, or political instability.
- Understand how rituals and ceremonies within a culture either alleviate or intensify collective anxiety.
- Investigate how cultural expectations and gender roles contribute to fear dynamics within a society.
- Explore case studies of cultures that have effectively managed and transformed collective fears over time.

Action Steps:
- Engage in workshops or programs to enhance cultural sensitivity and understanding.
- Foster open discussions within communities to explore and challenge cultural fears.
- Encourage the sharing of personal narratives within cultural contexts to promote empathy and understanding.
- Participate in or support programs that facilitate cultural exchange, broadening perspectives.
- Initiate campaigns that highlight the impact of cultural factors on mental health and collective anxiety.

2. Media Influence on Collective Anxiety:
Overviews:
- Media, including traditional and social platforms, has a profound impact on shaping collective fears and anxieties.
- Sensationalized reporting, misinformation, and the constant stream of negative news contribute to heightened societal anxiety.
- Social media's role in amplifying fears through viral content and online discussions requires critical examination.
- Media's influence on fear extends beyond news to entertainment, advertising, and popular culture.
- Recognizing the responsibility of media outlets in mitigating rather than exacerbating collective anxiety is crucial.

Explorations:
- Explore the psychological mechanisms through which media consumption influences fear responses.
- Examine case studies where media coverage either alleviated or intensified collective fears during crises.
- Understand the impact of social media algorithms on the spread and reinforcement of fear-inducing content.
- Investigate the role of storytelling in movies, television, and literature in perpetuating or challenging societal fears.

- Explore initiatives and media campaigns that aim to promote positive narratives and counterbalance fear-inducing content.

Action Steps:
- Advocate for and participate in programs that enhance media literacy skills within communities.
- Develop habits of consuming diverse, positive, and balanced media content.
- Engage in or organize workshops to critically analyze media messages and narratives.
- Support and promote initiatives calling for responsible and ethical media reporting.
- Encourage the creation of community-driven media projects that highlight positive aspects and solutions.

3. Collective Trauma and Societal Anxiety:

Overviews:
- Collective traumas, such as wars, pandemics, or natural disasters, leave lasting imprints on societal psyche, contributing to collective anxiety.
- Understanding the long-term effects of historical traumas on current generations helps address present anxieties.
- The transmission of trauma through generations requires acknowledgment and targeted interventions.
- Collective healing involves acknowledging and addressing the impact of historical injustices and traumas.

Explorations:
- Explore case studies of societies that successfully navigated collective trauma and minimized long-term anxiety.
- Examine the role of cultural rituals and practices in the healing process after collective traumas.
- Understand how governments and institutions acknowledge and address historical traumas to promote healing.
- Investigate the impact of art, literature, and cultural expressions in processing and transcending collective trauma.
- Explore psychological models for addressing collective trauma and preventing its negative impact on societal mental health.

Action Steps:
- Advocate for trauma-informed education programs to increase awareness and understanding.
- Create safe spaces for communities to collectively process and heal from historical traumas.
- Facilitate intergenerational dialogues to bridge understanding and promote healing.
- Support policies that acknowledge and address historical injustices, promoting societal healing.
- Contribute to initiatives that preserve and celebrate cultural practices that aid in collective healing.

4. Fear of Otherness: Navigating Cultural Differences:

Overviews:
- Fear of otherness arises from the unfamiliarity or perceived threat associated with different cultures, ethnicities, or identities.
- Stereotypes, prejudice, and xenophobia contribute to the fear of otherness, impacting social cohesion.
- Cultural diversity should be celebrated as a source of enrichment rather than viewed through a lens of fear.
- Understanding the root causes of the fear of otherness helps dismantle discriminatory attitudes and behaviors.
- Fostering empathy and building bridges across diverse cultures is essential for reducing the fear of otherness.

Explorations:
- Explore historical instances where fear of otherness led to societal tensions and conflicts.
- Examine the role of media and cultural narratives in perpetuating stereotypes that contribute to the fear of otherness.
- Understand the psychological processes that underlie the fear of the unknown and unfamiliar.
- Investigate successful initiatives and policies that promote cultural understanding and mitigate the fear of otherness.

Action Steps:
- Actively participate in or support cultural exchange programs to broaden perspectives.
- Advocate for anti-bias education in schools and community settings to address stereotypes.

- Engage in dialogues that promote understanding and respect among people from different cultural and religious backgrounds.
- Organize events that celebrate cultural diversity and foster a sense of community.
- Advocate for diverse and authentic representation in media to challenge stereotypes and reduce the fear of otherness.

5. Cultural Practices for Anxiety Alleviation:

Overviews:
- Many cultures have traditional practices that serve as effective tools for alleviating anxiety and promoting mental well-being.
- Rituals, ceremonies, and communal activities play a significant role in fostering a sense of belonging and security.
- Integrating cultural practices into modern lifestyles can provide a holistic approach to anxiety management.
- The preservation and adaptation of cultural practices contribute to the resilience of communities in the face of collective anxieties.
- Recognizing the diversity of cultural approaches to anxiety alleviation allows for a more inclusive and comprehensive understanding.

Explorations:
- Explore traditional ceremonies and rituals that are specifically designed to address anxiety and fear within various cultures.
- Examine the role of community support and solidarity in traditional cultural practices for anxiety alleviation.
- Understand the connection between cultural practices, spirituality, and mental well-being.
- Investigate how modern therapeutic practices can integrate and learn from traditional cultural approaches to anxiety management.
- Explore the impact of globalization on the preservation and adaptation of cultural practices for anxiety alleviation.

Action Steps:
- Organize workshops that facilitate the integration of traditional cultural practices into modern lifestyles.
- Create spaces within communities where traditional practices for anxiety alleviation can be shared and practiced.
- Encourage the exchange of knowledge and practices among different cultural groups for mutual enrichment.
- Contribute to initiatives that aim to preserve and protect traditional cultural practices related to anxiety alleviation.
- Promote educational programs that highlight the diversity of cultural approaches to mental well-being.

Chapter 33

Learning from Leaders:
Biographical Tales of Overcoming Fear

1. The Power of Inspirational Leadership Stories:
Overviews:
- Biographical tales of leaders overcoming fear provide powerful narratives that inspire and resonate with a diverse audience.
- These stories often highlight the vulnerability and humanity of leaders, making their triumphs over fear more relatable.
- Leaders' accounts of fear and resilience can serve as valuable lessons for individuals facing similar challenges.
- The impact of leadership stories extends beyond personal motivation, influencing organizational cultures and societal perceptions.
- Studying how leaders navigate fear offers insights into the qualities and strategies that contribute to their success.

Explorations:
- Explore biographies and autobiographies of leaders from various fields, focusing on their encounters with fear.
- Examine the role of self-awareness in leaders' ability to confront and overcome fears.
- Understand the influence of mentors, role models, and support networks in leaders' fear management journeys.
- Investigate how leaders leverage fear as a catalyst for growth and innovation.
- Analyze the societal impact of leaders who openly share their struggles with fear, destigmatizing vulnerability.

Action Steps:
- Establish book clubs or discussion groups centered around leadership biographies.
- Facilitate mentorship initiatives that connect emerging leaders with experienced mentors.
- Create platforms for leaders to share their personal stories of overcoming fear.
- Conduct workshops that integrate lessons from leadership stories into professional development.
- Advocate for the inclusion of leadership stories in educational curricula to inspire future generations.

2. Building Resilience Through Adversity:
Overviews:
- Leaders often face significant adversity, and their responses to challenges contribute to their leadership narratives.
- Adversity fosters resilience, and leaders who navigate fear-inducing situations emerge stronger and more capable.
- Examining how leaders bounce back from setbacks provides valuable insights into the cultivation of resilience.
- Personal and professional growth resulting from adversity contributes to leaders' ability to guide others through fear.
- The journey of overcoming adversity becomes a foundational aspect of leaders' identities and leadership styles.

Explorations:
- Explore case studies of leaders who turned setbacks into opportunities for personal and professional growth.
- Examine the psychological mechanisms behind resilience and its role in fear management.
- Understand how leaders maintain focus and determination during challenging times.
- Investigate the ripple effects of leaders' resilience on the organizational and community levels.
- Analyze the balance between vulnerability and strength in leaders' narratives of overcoming adversity.

Action Steps:
- Integrate resilience-building programs into leadership development initiatives.

- Organize workshops that explore strategies for transforming adversity into growth.
- Facilitate retreats where leaders can reflect on their experiences and share insights.
- Implement mental health resources and support networks for leaders facing adversity.
- Establish awards or recognitions for leaders who demonstrate exceptional resilience.

3. Strategies for Fear Management in Leadership:

Overviews:
- Effective leaders employ diverse strategies for managing fear, contributing to their success in challenging roles.
- Examining the tactical approaches leaders use to confront fear provides practical insights for others.
- These strategies encompass emotional intelligence, effective communication, and decision-making under uncertainty.
- The adaptability of leaders in the face of fear often involves a combination of proactive and reactive measures.
- Understanding the role of continuous learning and self-reflection in fear management is crucial for aspiring leaders.

Explorations:
- Explore case studies of leaders who demonstrate exceptional emotional intelligence in fear-inducing situations.
- Examine communication strategies employed by leaders to address and alleviate fear within their teams.
- Understand decision-making frameworks that leaders use to navigate uncertainty and mitigate fear.
- Investigate how leaders balance vulnerability with authority in their interactions with team members.
- Analyze the impact of ongoing learning and adaptability on leaders' ability to manage evolving fears.

Action Steps:
- Develop programs that teach emotional intelligence and communication skills to emerging leaders.
- Conduct workshops focusing on effective decision-making in high-pressure situations.
- Establish networks where leaders can share strategies for fear management.
- Implement feedback mechanisms to help leaders understand their impact on team members.
- Provide coaching services that support leaders in refining their fear management strategies.

4. Ethical Leadership in the Face of Fear:

Overviews:
- Leaders are often confronted with ethical dilemmas that evoke fear of making the wrong choices.
- Examining how leaders navigate ethical challenges provides insights into the intersection of fear and morality.
- Ethical leadership involves prioritizing values and principles over immediate gains, requiring courage in decision-making.
- The impact of leaders' ethical choices on organizational culture and societal trust is a critical aspect of leadership narratives.
- Leaders who prioritize ethical considerations in the face of fear contribute to long-term organizational sustainability.

Explorations:
- Explore historical and contemporary examples of leaders facing ethical challenges and fear.
- Examine the psychological factors that contribute to fear when making ethically significant decisions.
- Understand the role of organizational culture in shaping leaders' ethical frameworks and fear responses.
- Investigate how leaders balance the short-term consequences of decisions with long-term ethical considerations.
- Analyze the public perception and trust in organizations led by leaders who prioritize ethical values.

Action Steps:
- Implement training programs that focus on ethical decision-making in leadership roles.
- Establish committees within organizations to provide guidance on ethical dilemmas.
- Implement transparent practices that hold leaders accountable for ethical decisions.
- Involve stakeholders in ethical decision-making processes to ensure diverse perspectives.
- Recognize and celebrate leaders who prioritize ethics in the face of fear.

5. Leadership in Times of Crisis:

Overviews:

- Crisis situations amplify fear, requiring leaders to demonstrate effective crisis leadership skills.
- Examining how leaders navigate crises provides lessons in maintaining composure and instilling confidence.
- Crisis leadership involves swift decision-making, clear communication, and a focus on collective well-being.
- Leaders who emerge as beacons of stability during crises leave a lasting impact on organizational resilience.
- The integration of empathy and decisiveness distinguishes exceptional crisis leaders from their counterparts.

- **Explorations:**
  - Explore case studies of leaders who successfully led teams through crises, addressing fear and uncertainty.
  - Examine communication strategies employed by leaders to provide reassurance and guidance during crises.
  - Understand the psychological impact of crisis leadership on leaders and their teams.
  - Investigate the role of empathy in leaders' decision-making processes during times of crisis.

Action Steps:

- Develop training programs that equip leaders with crisis management skills.
- Conduct crisis simulation exercises to prepare leaders for real-time challenges.
- Provide mental health resources for leaders and teams navigating crises.
- Facilitate reflective sessions for leaders to learn from crisis experiences and adapt strategies.
- Acknowledge and reward leaders who demonstrate exceptional leadership during crises.

Chapter 34

The Spirituality of Fearlessness:
Exploring Inner Dimensions

1. Understanding the Spiritual Foundations of Fearlessness:
Overviews:

- The spirituality of fearlessness involves a deep exploration of inner dimensions, seeking tranquility and resilience.
- Spiritual practices form a foundation for cultivating fearlessness, transcending the limitations of the ego and material concerns.
- Leaders often draw strength from spiritual beliefs, guiding them through challenges with a profound sense of purpose.
- The exploration of inner dimensions encompasses mindfulness, meditation, and a connection to a higher purpose.
- The integration of spirituality and fearlessness fosters a holistic approach to leadership and personal development.

Explorations:

- Explore various spiritual traditions and their teachings on overcoming fear and cultivating fearlessness.
- Examine how leaders incorporate spiritual practices into their daily lives and decision-making processes.
- Understand the role of mindfulness in spirituality and its impact on fear perception and management.
- Investigate the connection between purpose-driven leadership and spiritual principles.
- Reflect on the intersection of spirituality, compassion, and fearlessness in leadership narratives.

Action Steps:

- Offer workshops on mindfulness practices, emphasizing their connection to fearlessness.
- Facilitate retreats that provide leaders with opportunities for spiritual reflection and growth.
- Encourage leaders to align their decision-making with spiritual values and principles.
- Organize seminars where leaders share how spirituality contributes to their fearlessness.
- Establish mentorship programs connecting leaders with spiritual guides for guidance.

2. Exploring Inner Transformation through Contemplative Practices:
Overviews:

- Contemplative practices, such as meditation and self-reflection, serve as gateways to inner transformation and fearlessness.
- Leaders who engage in these practices often exhibit enhanced emotional regulation and resilience.
- Inner transformation involves transcending self-limiting beliefs and developing a heightened awareness of one's inner world.
- The journey of inner exploration contributes to leaders' abilities to navigate external challenges with grace and composure.
- Contemplative practices offer a pathway to accessing intuitive wisdom and fostering a deeper understanding of fear.

Explorations:

- Explore different contemplative practices and their effects on the brain, emotions, and overall well-being.
- Examine how leaders integrate contemplative practices into their leadership styles and decision-making processes.
- Understand the relationship between self-awareness cultivated through contemplation and fear management.
- Investigate the impact of regular contemplative practices on stress reduction and mental clarity in leadership roles.
- Reflect on the interconnectedness of contemplative practices and the development of emotional intelligence.

Action Steps:

- Implement programs that teach leaders various contemplative practices.
- Develop courses that explore the intersection of mindfulness, leadership, and fearlessness.
- Organize retreats where leaders engage in reflective practices to enhance self-awareness.
- Provide coaching services that integrate contemplative techniques into leadership development.

3. Embracing Vulnerability and Authenticity in Leadership:

Overviews:

- Fearlessness in a spiritual context involves embracing vulnerability and authenticity as sources of strength.
- Leaders who authentically acknowledge their fears create a culture of openness and trust within their teams.
- Authenticity fosters genuine connections, allowing leaders to relate to the human experiences of those they lead.
- The willingness to be vulnerable contributes to leaders' relatability and resilience, inspiring others to confront their fears.
- Spiritual teachings often emphasize the transformative power of vulnerability and authenticity in leadership.

Explorations:

- Explore how leaders incorporate vulnerability and authenticity into their leadership narratives and communication styles.
- Examine the role of humility in spiritual traditions and its connection to fearlessness in leadership.
- Understand the impact of leaders' openness about their fears on team dynamics and organizational culture.
- Investigate the relationship between authentic leadership and the ability to navigate uncertainty and ambiguity.
- Reflect on how spiritual principles guide leaders in finding strength in vulnerability and authenticity.

Action Steps:

- Facilitate workshops that explore the intersection of authenticity, spirituality, and fearlessness.
- Integrate modules on vulnerability and authenticity into leadership development programs.
- Create spaces where leaders can share authentic stories about their fear management journeys.
- Encourage leaders to cultivate humility through practices such as self-reflection and seeking feedback.

4. Nurturing Compassion as a Catalyst for Fearlessness:

Overviews:

- Compassion, rooted in spiritual principles, serves as a catalyst for fearlessness by fostering empathy and understanding.
- Leaders who prioritize compassion create supportive environments that empower individuals to face fears collectively.
- Compassionate leadership involves acknowledging and alleviating the fears of team members with empathy and kindness.
- The connection between spirituality and compassion reinforces the idea that fearlessness is intertwined with caring for others.
- Nurturing compassion within leadership leads to a ripple effect of fearlessness throughout an organization.

Explorations:

- Explore spiritual teachings on compassion and their applications in modern leadership practices.
- Examine how compassionate leaders approach fear management within themselves and their teams.
- Understand the impact of compassionate leadership on employee well-being, satisfaction, and fear reduction.
- Investigate the role of self-compassion in leaders' ability to navigate personal fears and challenges.
- Reflect on how compassion contributes to a culture of trust, collaboration, and fearlessness.

Action Steps:

- Host seminars that delve into the intersection of spirituality, compassion, and fearlessness in leadership.
- Provide training programs that teach leaders practical methods for cultivating compassion.
- Conduct workshops on compassionate communication, emphasizing its role in fear management.

- Organize retreats focused on building compassion within teams to create a supportive work environment.
- Implement recognition initiatives that highlight and reward acts of compassion within the organization.

5. Integrating Fearless Values into Organizational Culture:

Overviews:

- Fearlessness, grounded in spirituality, extends beyond individual leaders to become embedded in organizational culture.
- Values such as integrity, authenticity, and compassion form the pillars of a fearless organizational culture.
- Organizations with a fearlessness-oriented culture foster innovation, resilience, and a shared sense of purpose.
- The alignment of organizational values with spiritual principles creates a harmonious and empowering work environment.
- Integrating fearless values into the organizational fabric inspires collective courage and a commitment to growth.

Explorations:

- Explore how organizational leaders infuse spiritual values into their organizational culture.
- Examine the impact of fearless organizational values on employee engagement, satisfaction, and performance.
- Understand how organizations can address and overcome challenges in aligning with spiritual principles.
- Investigate the role of leadership in sustaining a fearless culture during times of change and uncertainty.
- Reflect on case studies of organizations that have successfully integrated spiritual values into their cultures.

Action Steps:

- Facilitate workshops to help organizations align their values with fearless principles.
- Organize retreats for leadership teams to collectively define and embody fearless values.
- Implement training programs that educate employees on the importance of fearless values.
- Establish feedback mechanisms to assess and reinforce the integration of fearless values.
- Introduce recognition programs that celebrate individuals and teams embodying fearless values in the organization.

Chapter 35

Rituals and Routines:
The Daily Practice of Fearless Living

1. Social Fears and Public Life: Finding Comfort in Community:
Overviews:
- Social fears encompass a range of anxieties related to social interactions, judgment, and rejection.
- Finding comfort in community involves creating supportive social networks that understand and accept individual differences.
- Addressing social fears contributes to enhanced self-esteem, increased social engagement, and improved well-being.
- Social fears can manifest in various settings, including social events, work environments, and online platforms.
- Building resilience against social fears requires a combination of self-awareness and active social participation.

Explorations:
- Reflect on specific social situations that trigger fear or anxiety and explore their origins.
- Examine societal expectations and cultural norms that influence social fears.
- Understand the impact of technology and social media on social fears and self-perception.
- Explore strategies for effective communication and assertiveness to navigate social situations confidently.
- Investigate the role of empathy and compassion in fostering supportive social connections.

Action Steps:
- Gradually expose oneself to social situations, starting with small and comfortable settings.
- Practice mindfulness and self-compassion techniques to manage social anxiety in the moment.
- Seek out social groups or communities that share common interests or values.
- Develop effective communication skills through workshops or interpersonal training.
- Collaborate with a mental health professional to address and overcome social fears through therapy or counseling.

2. The Fear of Unknown: Embracing Uncertainty:
Overviews:
- Fear of the unknown, or uncertainty, is a common human experience with both psychological and physiological implications.
- Embracing uncertainty involves cultivating a mindset that views the unknown as an opportunity for growth and learning.
- Uncertainty can trigger anxiety, and managing this fear requires resilience and adaptability.
- Exploring the positive aspects of uncertainty can lead to increased creativity and a sense of adventure.
- Resisting the urge to control every aspect of life and acknowledging the inevitability of uncertainty is key to fear management.

Explorations:
- Reflect on specific areas of life where the fear of the unknown is prevalent and examine underlying beliefs.
- Explore cultural and societal attitudes toward uncertainty and how they shape individual perspectives.
- Understand the relationship between fear of the unknown and the desire for control.
- Examine historical or personal experiences that have influenced the perception of uncertainty.
- Explore philosophical perspectives on uncertainty and its role in the human experience.

Action Steps:
- Practice mindfulness and grounding techniques to stay present in uncertain moments.
- Gradually expose oneself to situations with varying degrees of uncertainty to build resilience.
- Challenge negative beliefs about uncertainty through cognitive-behavioral techniques.
- Engage in activities that foster a sense of curiosity and openness to new experiences.

- Seek guidance from mentors or role models who have embraced uncertainty and thrived in ambiguous situations.

3.Fear and Finances: Tackling Money-Related Worries:

Overviews:

- Fear related to finances can significantly impact mental well-being and overall quality of life.
- Tackling money-related worries involves a combination of financial literacy, budgeting, and emotional regulation.
- Addressing the fear of financial instability requires understanding and reframing beliefs about money.
- Financial fears may stem from societal pressures, comparison, or past experiences, necessitating exploration.
- Developing a healthy relationship with money involves both practical financial management and emotional resilience.

Explorations:

- Reflect on personal beliefs and attitudes toward money and how they contribute to financial fears.
- Explore the impact of societal expectations and cultural influences on financial anxieties.
- Understand the connection between financial fears and broader concerns about security and well-being.
- Examine the role of financial education and literacy in building confidence and reducing fear.
- Investigate the relationship between self-worth and financial success or stability.

Action Steps:

- Create a realistic budget and financial plan to gain a clearer understanding of one's financial situation.
- Seek guidance from financial professionals or advisors to address specific concerns and questions.
- Gradually confront financial fears by taking small, manageable steps toward financial goals.
- Practice gratitude for current financial circumstances, fostering a positive outlook.
- Engage in ongoing financial education to empower oneself with knowledge and skills for effective money management.

4.The Adventurer's Mindset: Fear as a Catalyst for Growth:

Overviews:

- Embracing fear as a catalyst for growth involves adopting an adventurer's mindset toward challenges.
- Viewing fear as a natural part of the growth process allows individuals to approach challenges with resilience.
- The adventurer's mindset involves reframing fear as an opportunity for learning, development, and self-discovery.
- Seeking out new experiences, taking calculated risks, and stepping outside comfort zones are key aspects of this mindset.
- Embracing uncertainty and seeing challenges as adventures can lead to a more fulfilling and expansive life.

Explorations:

- Reflect on past experiences where facing fear led to personal growth and positive outcomes.
- Explore the concept of the growth mindset and its relationship to viewing challenges as opportunities.
- Understand the role of curiosity and a sense of adventure in overcoming fear.
- Examine personal values and aspirations to align them with a growth-oriented mindset.
- Investigate the stories of individuals who have embraced fear as a catalyst for transformative experiences.

Action Steps:

- Identify and set intentional growth-oriented goals that align with personal values.
- Challenge the fear of failure by reframing setbacks as opportunities for learning and improvement.
- Engage in activities that push personal boundaries and expand comfort zones.
- Surround oneself with a supportive community that encourages taking risks and pursuing growth.
- Practice self-compassion and celebrate the journey of personal growth, recognizing the courage it takes to face fears.

5.Creativity's Antidote to Fear: Using Art to Heal:

Overviews:

- Creativity serves as a powerful antidote to fear, offering a means of self-expression, catharsis, and healing.

- Engaging in artistic endeavors allows individuals to process and communicate complex emotions related to fear.
- The creative process fosters self-discovery, providing insights into the roots of fear and potential avenues for healing.
- Various forms of art, including visual arts, writing, music, and dance, can be utilized as therapeutic tools for fear management.
- Embracing creativity as an antidote to fear involves both the process of creation and the appreciation of artistic expressions.

Explorations:
- Reflect on personal experiences of using art as a means of coping with or expressing fear.
- Explore different forms of art that resonate with individual preferences and interests.
- Understand the psychological and emotional impact of engaging in the creative process.
- Examine how art can serve as a tool for narrative transformation and reframing fear-based stories.
- Investigate the connection between creativity, mindfulness, and emotional well-being.

- **Action Steps:**
  - Incorporate regular creative practices into daily or weekly routines for self-expression and emotional release.
  - Attend art classes, workshops, or join creative communities to enhance artistic skills and share experiences.
  - Use art as a tool for self-reflection, exploring themes related to fear and resilience.
  - Share creative works with others, fostering connection and understanding through artistic expression.
  - Explore art therapy or counseling to delve deeper into the therapeutic benefits of creative expression.

.

Chapter 36

The Hero's Journey:
Your Path Through Fear

1.The Hero's Journey: Your Path Through Fear:
Overviews:

* The hero's journey serves as a metaphor for the transformative process individuals undergo when facing and conquering fear.
* Recognizing fear as a call to adventure, the hero's journey invites individuals to embark on a path of self-discovery and growth.
* Each stage of the hero's journey, from the initial call to adventure to the return with newfound wisdom, mirrors the phases of fear management.
* Embracing the hero's journey framework empowers individuals to view fears as challenges and opportunities for personal development.
* The hero's journey highlights the universal nature of overcoming fear and the archetypal narratives that guide individuals through their own quests.

Explorations:

* Reflect on personal experiences of fear, identifying key stages that align with the hero's journey.
* Explore archetypal stories and myths that resonate with the journey of overcoming fear, recognizing common themes.
* Examine the role of mentors, allies, and obstacles in the hero's journey and their parallels in fear management.
* Understand the psychological and emotional transformations that occur at each stage of the hero's journey.

Action Steps:

* Map out the stages of the hero's journey, aligning them with specific fears or challenges.
* Identify mentors or role models who embody qualities that inspire courage and resilience.
* Create a visual representation of the hero's journey, incorporating personal symbols and milestones.
* Journal about the emotional and psychological shifts experienced at each stage of fear management.

2.The Resilient Mind: Nurturing Mental Toughness
Overviews:

* Resilience is the capacity to bounce back from adversity, and mental toughness is a key component of this psychological strength.
* Developing a resilient mind involves cultivating habits, perspectives, and coping mechanisms that enhance adaptive responses to challenges.
* Mental toughness is characterized by a positive mindset, focus, emotional regulation, and a commitment to personal growth.
* Resilience and mental toughness contribute to fear management by providing a solid foundation for facing and overcoming challenges.

Explorations:

* Explore the characteristics of mentally tough individuals, including their mindset, habits, and response to setbacks.
* Reflect on past experiences of resilience, identifying the factors and strategies that contributed to overcoming adversity.
* Examine the connection between a positive mindset, emotional regulation, and the ability to navigate fear effectively.
* Understand the role of self-talk and cognitive reframing in building mental toughness and resilience.
* Investigate the concept of post-traumatic growth and how overcoming fear can lead to personal development and positive transformation.

Action Steps:

* Cultivate a growth mindset by embracing challenges as opportunities for learning and improvement.

- Develop a daily gratitude practice to foster a positive outlook and enhance emotional well-being.
- Establish a routine of mindfulness and meditation to build emotional regulation and mental clarity.
- Set specific, achievable goals that align with personal values, fostering a sense of purpose and direction.
- Seek out mentorship or coaching to receive guidance on building mental toughness and developing resilience.

3.Courageous Vulnerability: Embracing Authenticity in the Face of Fear

Overviews:

- Courageous vulnerability involves the willingness to be authentic, open, and honest about one's fears and imperfections.
- Authenticity creates connections with others, fostering empathy and understanding in shared human experiences of fear.
- Embracing vulnerability is a courageous act that challenges societal expectations and promotes genuine connections.
- Authentic self-expression in the face of fear allows individuals to break free from societal norms and embrace their unique journey.

Explorations:

- Reflect on personal experiences of vulnerability and authenticity, considering the impact on fear management.
- Explore societal norms and expectations around vulnerability, identifying areas where authenticity is suppressed.
- Examine the connection between self-acceptance, vulnerability, and the ability to navigate fear with resilience.
- Understand the role of empathy and shared vulnerability in building supportive communities.
- Investigate the concept of radical authenticity, where individuals unapologetically embrace their true selves in the face of fear.

Action Steps:

- Practice vulnerability by sharing fears and insecurities with trusted friends, family, or support groups.
- Challenge societal expectations by embracing and expressing aspects of yourself that defy conventional norms.
- Foster empathy by actively listening to others' stories of fear and vulnerability without judgment.
- Create a safe space for authentic self-expression in personal and professional relationships.
- Lead by example in embracing courageous vulnerability, inspiring others to share their authentic selves.

4.The Mind-Body Connection: Holistic Approaches to Fear Management

Overviews:

- The mind-body connection emphasizes the interdependence of mental and physical well-being in fear management.
- Holistic approaches involve integrating mental, emotional, and physical practices to enhance overall resilience.
- Techniques such as mindfulness, yoga, and breathwork contribute to a balanced mind-body connection, promoting fear resilience.
- Nutrition, sleep, and lifestyle factors also play a crucial role in supporting a healthy mind-body balance in the face of fear.
- Holistic approaches recognize the dynamic relationship between thoughts, emotions, and physical sensations in fear responses.

Explorations:

- Explore various mind-body practices, such as mindfulness meditation, and observe their impact on fear perception.
- Reflect on the connection between physical well-being, stress levels, and the experience of fear.
- Examine the role of nutrition and hydration in supporting cognitive function and emotional regulation during fear.
- Understand the impact of sleep quality on fear resilience and overall mental health.
- Investigate the science behind mind-body practices, including their influence on neurotransmitters and stress hormones.

Action Steps:

- Incorporate daily mindfulness or meditation practices to enhance self-awareness and emotional regulation.
- Engage in regular physical activity that aligns with personal preferences, promoting a healthy mind-body balance.
- Adopt a balanced and nutritious diet, emphasizing foods that support cognitive function and mood stability.
- Prioritize regular and sufficient sleep, aiming for 7-9 hours per night.

5.The Power of Rituals: Cultivating Fearlessness in Daily Life

Overviews:

- Rituals play a significant role in cultivating fearlessness by providing structure, meaning, and a sense of continuity in daily life.
- Establishing intentional rituals contributes to a sense of stability and control, counteracting the disruptive influence of fear.
- Rituals can range from simple daily practices to more elaborate ceremonies, offering individuals a tangible way to connect with their values.
- Consistent engagement in rituals fosters a positive mindset, resilience, and a heightened awareness of the present moment.

Explorations:

- Reflect on existing rituals in your life and their impact on your emotional well-being and fear management.
- Explore various types of rituals, including personal, familial, cultural, and spiritual, to understand their diversity and significance.
- Examine the psychological mechanisms behind rituals and their ability to create a sense of security and meaning.
- Understand the role of intentionality in ritual creation and how it enhances the fearlessness cultivated through these practices.

Action Steps:

- Establish a daily routine that includes intentional rituals aligned with your values and aspirations.
- Create a personal ritual to mark significant life events or transitions, fostering a sense of closure and new beginnings.
- Incorporate mindfulness practices into existing rituals, enhancing your awareness and presence during these moments.
- Explore cultural or spiritual rituals that resonate with you, providing a sense of connection to broader traditions.
- Share meaningful rituals with friends or family, building a collective sense of purpose and fearlessness in daily life.

Chapter 37

Acknowledging Progress:
Celebrating Victories Over Fear

1. Acknowledging Progress: Celebrating Victories Over Fear
Overviews:
- Recognizing and celebrating progress in overcoming fears is essential for personal growth and well-being.
- Acknowledging progress involves reflecting on achievements, no matter how small, in the journey of conquering fears.
- Celebrating victories over fear reinforces a positive mindset, boosting confidence and self-esteem.
- Progress recognition is a continuous process, fostering resilience by highlighting one's capacity for growth.
- Acknowledging progress creates a forward-looking perspective, emphasizing the potential for future successes.

Explorations:
- Reflect on personal experiences of overcoming fears and identify the associated achievements.
- Explore the psychological impact of acknowledging progress on overall mental well-being.
- Examine the role of external validation versus internal acknowledgment in the process of celebrating victories.
- Investigate cultural variations in recognizing and celebrating achievements related to overcoming fears.
- Understand the connection between acknowledging progress and cultivating a mindset of gratitude.

Action Steps:
- Engage in daily or weekly gratitude journaling to reflect on and acknowledge progress.
- Establish personal rituals or ceremonies to celebrate victories over specific fears.
- Join or create support groups where individuals can share and celebrate their triumphs.
- Encourage public acknowledgment of personal achievements to inspire others.
- Initiate or participate in mentorship programs where individuals guide each other in recognizing and celebrating progress.

2. Embracing Vulnerability: The Strength in Openness
Overviews:
- Embracing vulnerability involves recognizing and accepting one's emotional openness and authentic self.
- Vulnerability is a source of strength, fostering deeper connections with oneself and others.
- The courage to be vulnerable allows for genuine self-expression and contributes to personal authenticity.
- Accepting vulnerability is essential for navigating and overcoming various fears, promoting resilience.
- Vulnerability serves as a catalyst for personal and interpersonal growth, creating opportunities for empathy and understanding.

Explorations:
- Reflect on personal experiences of vulnerability and explore the impact on self-awareness and relationships.
- Examine societal perceptions of vulnerability and how they influence individual willingness to be open.
- Explore the link between vulnerability, trust, and the quality of relationships in personal and professional spheres.
- Investigate cultural attitudes towards vulnerability and expressions of openness in different societies.
- Understand the role of vulnerability in fostering creativity, innovation, and adaptive responses to fear.

Action Steps:
- Participate in workshops or therapy sessions focused on embracing vulnerability.

- Cultivate open communication by expressing thoughts and feelings authentically.
- Build or join communities that encourage vulnerability and provide a safe space for openness.
- Seek mentorship from individuals who exemplify the strength of vulnerability.
- Advocate for the destigmatization of vulnerability in societal narratives through public discussions and campaigns.

3. The Power of Self-Compassion: Nurturing Kindness Within

Overviews:
- Self-compassion involves treating oneself with kindness, understanding, and acceptance during times of struggle or failure.
- Cultivating self-compassion is essential for building emotional resilience and reducing the impact of fear on mental well-being.
- Recognizing shared human experiences in suffering helps individuals develop a sense of common humanity through self-compassion.
- The practice of self-compassion involves being mindful of one's thoughts and emotions without judgment.
- Nurturing a self-compassionate mindset contributes to increased self-esteem and a positive outlook on life.

Explorations:
- Reflect on personal experiences of self-compassion and its influence on emotional well-being.
- Explore cultural and societal attitudes towards self-compassion and self-care practices.
- Examine the connection between self-compassion and the ability to cope with various fears and anxieties.
- Investigate therapeutic approaches and interventions that incorporate self-compassion for mental health.
- Understand how self-compassion contributes to healthier relationships and improved overall life satisfaction.

Action Steps:
- Engage in mindfulness meditation and activities to enhance self-awareness and self-compassion.
- Start a journal to regularly express self-compassionate thoughts and reflections.
- Consult with mental health professionals who incorporate self-compassion in their therapeutic approaches.
- Establish daily practices that prioritize self-care and self-compassion.
- Participate in or organize workshops that promote self-compassion within communities.

4. The Role of Mindfulness in Fear Management: Cultivating Present-Moment Awareness

Overviews:
- Mindfulness involves cultivating a heightened awareness of the present moment without judgment.
- Integrating mindfulness practices into daily life contributes to a more balanced and centered approach to fear.
- Mindfulness allows individuals to observe their thoughts and emotions, fostering a non-reactive mindset.
- The practice of mindfulness is rooted in ancient contemplative traditions and has gained recognition in modern psychological therapies.
- Developing mindfulness skills enhances emotional regulation and resilience in the face of fear-inducing situations.

Explorations:
- Explore various mindfulness techniques such as meditation, mindful breathing, and body scans.
- Examine the scientific research supporting the effectiveness of mindfulness in reducing anxiety and fear.
- Understand how mindfulness can interrupt habitual fear responses and promote a sense of calm.
- Investigate mindfulness-based interventions for specific fears, such as phobias or trauma-related anxieties.
- Reflect on personal experiences of integrating mindfulness into daily routines and its impact on fear management.

Action Steps:
- Dedicate time each day to mindfulness exercises to build a consistent practice.

- Explore and utilize mindfulness apps that provide guided sessions and resources.
- Consider attending mindfulness retreats for immersive experiences and skill development.
- Practice mindfulness during routine activities like eating, walking, or commuting.
- Encourage others in your community to adopt mindfulness practices for fear management.

5. Courageous Vulnerability: Embracing Authenticity in the Face of Fear

Overviews:

- Courageous vulnerability involves the willingness to be authentic and open about one's fears and insecurities.
- Embracing vulnerability fosters connection with oneself and others, breaking down barriers created by fear.
- The courage to be vulnerable is rooted in the understanding that vulnerability is a strength, not a weakness.
- Authenticity in expressing fears allows for genuine human connection and supportive relationships.
- Courageous vulnerability is an empowering approach that encourages growth, resilience, and a sense of liberation.

Explorations:

- Explore personal experiences of vulnerability and its impact on relationships and self-perception.
- Examine societal attitudes towards vulnerability and how they influence the expression of fear.
- Understand the role of self-compassion in embracing vulnerability without self-judgment.
- Investigate how courageous vulnerability contributes to the creation of supportive and understanding communities.
- Reflect on the connection between vulnerability, creativity, and innovation in overcoming fears.

Action Steps:

- Openly share personal experiences of fear and vulnerability with trusted individuals.
- Attend workshops or engage in activities that explore and cultivate courageous vulnerability.
- Join support groups where individuals share their fears and vulnerabilities in a safe space.
- Encourage environments that value and support authenticity, openness, and vulnerability.
- Develop self-compassion as a foundation for embracing vulnerability and navigating fear authentically.

Chapter 38

Fear in Times of Crisis:
Coping Strategies for Tough Periods

1. Resilience as a Foundation in Times of Crisis: Building Inner Strength
Overviews:

- Resilience is the capacity to bounce back from adversity and maintain mental well-being during challenging times.
- Developing resilience involves cultivating a mindset that views challenges as opportunities for growth.
- Resilient individuals can adapt to change, manage stress effectively, and navigate uncertainties with a positive outlook.
- Building resilience is a proactive approach to fear management, equipping individuals to face crises with greater fortitude.
- Resilience is a skill that can be developed through various practices and strategies.

Explorations:

- Explore personal strengths and coping mechanisms that have helped in past challenging situations.
- Examine the role of mindset and perception in shaping resilience during times of crisis.
- Understand how social support and community connections contribute to individual and collective resilience.
- Investigate the impact of mindfulness, self-care, and positive psychology on building resilience.
- Reflect on the concept of post-traumatic growth and how crises can become catalysts for personal development.

Action Steps:

- Engage in resilience-building workshops or programs offered by mental health professionals.
- Incorporate mindfulness exercises into daily routines to enhance emotional resilience.
- Strengthen social connections and build a support network for times of crisis.
- Keep a journal to reflect on challenges, coping strategies, and personal growth.
- Develop a crisis management plan that includes coping strategies and resources for tough periods.

2. Emotional Intelligence in Crisis: Navigating and Understanding Emotions
Overviews:

- Emotional intelligence involves recognizing, understanding, and managing one's own emotions and those of others.
- During crises, emotions can run high, and developing emotional intelligence is crucial for effective fear management.
- Cultivating emotional intelligence enhances self-awareness, empathy, and the ability to make informed decisions under stress.
- Understanding the interplay between thoughts, emotions, and behaviors provides a foundation for resilient responses.
- Emotional intelligence fosters effective communication, collaboration, and relationship-building during tough times.

Explorations:

- Explore personal emotional responses to past crises and their impact on decision-making.
- Examine how societal and cultural factors influence the expression and management of emotions during crises.
- Understand the role of empathy in building connections and providing support during challenging periods.
- Investigate the impact of emotional intelligence on leadership effectiveness in times of crisis.
- Reflect on the connection between emotional well-being and overall resilience in the face of adversity.

Action Steps:

- Attend workshops or courses focused on developing emotional intelligence skills.
- Practice mindfulness meditation to enhance emotional awareness and regulation.

- Engage in activities that promote understanding and empathy towards others' experiences.
- Develop effective communication skills for navigating difficult conversations during crises.

3. Community Connection and Mutual Support: Collective Resilience Strategies

Overviews:
- Community connection and mutual support are integral aspects of collective resilience in times of crisis.
- Strong community bonds contribute to a sense of belonging, shared responsibility, and collective problem-solving.
- Communities with a high level of social cohesion are better equipped to face and overcome adversity.
- Mutual support involves individuals coming together to offer assistance, share resources, and provide emotional comfort.
- Building a resilient community involves fostering trust, open communication, and a culture of solidarity.

Explorations:
- Explore historical examples where communities demonstrated resilience through collective support.
- Examine the role of community leaders and organizers in facilitating mutual aid during crises.
- Understand how cultural and societal values influence the level of community connection and support.
- Investigate community-based initiatives that promote well-being and resilience during tough times.
- Reflect on personal experiences of community support and its impact on individual and collective resilience.

Action Steps:
- Participate in or organize activities that strengthen community bonds and connections.
- Create networks for mutual aid, resource-sharing, and emotional support within communities.
- Contribute time and effort to community service projects that address shared challenges.
- Utilize communication platforms to disseminate information, resources, and support within the community.
- Work with community members to develop contingency plans and strategies for collective resilience.

4. Adaptive Strategies for Uncertainty: Thriving in Ambiguity

Overviews:
- Adaptive strategies involve cultivating a mindset that embraces uncertainty and adapts to changing circumstances.
- The ability to thrive in ambiguity is crucial during crises when the future is often unpredictable.
- Adaptive individuals can adjust their goals, plans, and perspectives to navigate uncertainty effectively.
- Resilience in the face of ambiguity requires a combination of flexibility, creativity, and a proactive approach.
- Developing adaptive strategies involves continuous learning, innovation, and a willingness to experiment.

Explorations:
- Explore personal experiences of adapting to unexpected changes and the lessons learned from such situations.
- Examine how different cultures and societies approach and cope with uncertainty.
- Understand the psychological factors that contribute to the discomfort associated with uncertainty.
- Investigate case studies of organizations or communities that successfully adapted to unforeseen challenges.
- Reflect on the role of personal values and beliefs in shaping one's ability to thrive in ambiguity.

Action Steps:
- Cultivate a mindset of continuous learning and adaptability.
- Engage in scenario planning exercises to prepare for potential future uncertainties.
- Develop creative problem-solving skills to address challenges in innovative ways.
- Connect with individuals from diverse backgrounds to gain varied perspectives on uncertainty.
- Attend workshops focused on building resilience in the face of ambiguity.

5. Compassionate Leadership in Crisis: Fostering a Supportive Environment

Overviews:
- Compassionate leadership involves prioritizing the well-being of individuals and creating a supportive environment.

- Leaders who demonstrate empathy, understanding, and active listening contribute to a positive organizational culture.
- During crises, compassionate leadership fosters a sense of security, trust, and collaboration among team members.
- Compassionate leaders empower individuals to navigate fear by providing resources, guidance, and emotional support.
- Building a culture of compassion within organizations enhances resilience and contributes to long-term success.

Explorations:
- Explore examples of compassionate leadership in various contexts, including business, healthcare, and community organizations.
- Examine the impact of compassionate leadership on employee morale, productivity, and overall well-being.
- Understand the role of communication in expressing empathy and fostering a sense of psychological safety.
- Investigate the connection between compassionate leadership and organizational resilience during crises.
- Reflect on personal experiences with leaders who demonstrated compassion and its influence on fear management.

Action Steps:
- Attend leadership training programs that emphasize empathy, active listening, and compassion.
- Implement initiatives focused on employee well-being, mental health, and work-life balance.
- Schedule regular check-ins with team members to inquire about their well-being and offer support.
- Provide training in conflict resolution to address challenges and maintain a positive work environment.
- Acknowledge and celebrate the efforts and contributions of individuals within the organization.

Chapter **39**

Creating a Fearless Environment:
Safe Spaces for Growth

1. Cultivating Psychological Safety: The Foundation of a Fearless Environment
Overviews:
- Psychological safety is a critical component of creating a fearless environment, fostering open communication and risk-taking.
- In psychologically safe spaces, individuals feel confident expressing ideas, sharing concerns, and contributing without fear of judgment.
- Cultivating psychological safety involves building trust, promoting inclusivity, and valuing diverse perspectives.
- A fearless environment encourages individuals to embrace vulnerability and view mistakes as opportunities for learning and growth.
- Psychological safety positively impacts mental well-being, creativity, and overall team dynamics.

Explorations:
- Explore the role of leadership in establishing and maintaining psychological safety within teams and organizations.
- Examine the impact of psychological safety on innovation, problem-solving, and the ability to navigate uncertainty.
- Understand how cultural and organizational factors influence the perception and implementation of psychological safety.
- Investigate case studies of companies or teams that have successfully prioritized and integrated psychological safety.
- Reflect on personal experiences in environments where psychological safety was present or lacking.

Action Steps:
- Leaders should participate in workshops focused on fostering psychological safety within teams.
- Engage in team-building activities that promote trust, collaboration, and open communication.
- Ensure inclusivity in decision-making processes, valuing input from all team members.
- Establish mechanisms for regular feedback, creating a culture of continuous improvement.
- Encourage calculated risk-taking and celebrate efforts even when outcomes are uncertain.

2. Empowering through Education: Knowledge as a Catalyst for Fear Reduction
Overviews:
- Education and knowledge dissemination play a key role in demystifying fears, debunking myths, and promoting understanding.
- Informed individuals are better equipped to navigate uncertainties, make informed decisions, and manage fear effectively.
- Creating a fearless environment involves providing accessible, accurate, and culturally sensitive information.
- Knowledge empowers individuals to challenge stereotypes, address misconceptions, and foster a culture of curiosity.
- A commitment to ongoing education contributes to a dynamic and adaptable community capable of embracing change.

Explorations:
- Explore the impact of education on dispelling common fears and promoting a more informed mindset.
- Examine the role of educational institutions, community programs, and online resources in fear reduction.
- Understand the connection between knowledge acquisition, critical thinking, and fear management.
- Investigate the impact of media literacy education in reducing anxiety related to misinformation and sensationalism.
- Reflect on personal experiences where education played a role in transforming perspectives on fear.

Action Steps:
- Implement programs that bring educational resources to communities, focusing on relevant fear-related topics.
- Leverage online platforms to provide accessible courses and resources for fear management.
- Conduct workshops that address common fears, providing evidence-based information.
- Support initiatives that promote media literacy, enabling individuals to critically assess information.
- Encourage a culture of lifelong learning within communities, emphasizing the value of continuous education.

3. Inclusive Design of Physical Spaces: Creating Environments for All
Overviews:
- Inclusive design focuses on creating physical environments that accommodate diverse needs and promote a sense of belonging.
- Fear can be heightened in spaces that lack accessibility, inclusivity, and accommodations for various abilities and backgrounds.
- Inclusive design principles contribute to a fearless environment by ensuring that spaces are welcoming and comfortable for everyone.
- Consideration of diverse sensory experiences, mobility challenges, and cultural preferences is integral to inclusive design.
- A commitment to inclusivity reflects a broader societal shift towards valuing diversity and embracing differences.

Explorations:
- Explore examples of inclusive design in public spaces that contribute to fear reduction.
- Examine the psychological impact of inclusive environments on individuals with various abilities and backgrounds.
- Understand how cultural and societal norms influence the design of public spaces and contribute to feelings of inclusion or exclusion.
- Investigate case studies of organizations or cities that have successfully implemented inclusive design principles.
- Reflect on personal experiences in environments that either fostered or hindered a sense of inclusivity and safety.

Action Steps:
- Conduct audits of public spaces to assess and improve accessibility for individuals with diverse needs.
- Involve community members in the design process to ensure inclusivity and cultural sensitivity.
- Implement measures to create sensory-inclusive environments, considering various sensory needs.
- Provide training on cultural competency to architects, designers, and urban planners.

4. Fostering a Culture of Supportive Relationships: Social Connections for Fear Resilience
Overviews:
- Supportive relationships and social connections are essential for creating a fearless environment.
- Strong social ties provide a sense of security, emotional support, and a network for navigating challenges.
- Building a culture of supportive relationships involves fostering empathy, active listening, and mutual understanding.
- Fear can be alleviated through shared experiences, collaborative problem-solving, and a collective sense of belonging.
- Communities that prioritize and nurture supportive relationships are more resilient in the face of adversity.

Explorations:
- Explore the impact of social isolation on fear and mental well-being, especially during times of crisis.
- Examine cultural norms and practices that contribute to the formation of strong social bonds within communities.
- Understand the role of leadership in promoting a culture of collaboration, trust, and interpersonal support.
- Investigate case studies of communities that successfully built resilient networks of social support.
- Reflect on personal experiences of the role of social connections in fear management.

Action Steps:
- Organize events that facilitate community interaction, fostering connections and friendships.
- Establish support groups within communities to address shared challenges and fears.
- Implement mentorship programs that connect individuals for mutual guidance and support.
- Provide training on crisis intervention to community leaders and support networks.
- Promote a sense of interconnectedness and interdependence within the community, emphasizing the value of collective support.

5. Nurturing Emotional Intelligence: Building Resilience through Understanding Emotions

Overviews:
- Emotional intelligence is a key factor in creating a fearless environment, enabling individuals to understand and manage their emotions effectively.
- Individuals with high emotional intelligence can navigate fear, stress, and uncertainty with greater resilience.
- A fearless environment encourages the development of emotional intelligence at both individual and community levels.
- Emotional intelligence involves self-awareness, self-regulation, empathy, and effective communication.
- Fostering emotional intelligence contributes to a positive community culture, enhancing interpersonal relationships and conflict resolution.

Explorations:
- Explore the impact of emotional intelligence on individual and community well-being in various cultural contexts.
- Examine educational programs and initiatives that promote the development of emotional intelligence.
- Understand the role of leadership in modeling and fostering emotional intelligence within organizations and communities.
- Investigate the connection between emotional intelligence and effective fear management during crises or challenging times.

Action Steps:
- Offer workshops and training programs focused on developing emotional intelligence skills.
- Integrate emotional intelligence education into school and community curricula.
- Provide leadership development programs that emphasize the importance of emotional intelligence.
- Facilitate open dialogues within communities to explore and share emotional experiences.
- Establish peer mentoring programs that provide emotional support and guidance within communities.

Chapter 40

The Compassion Connection:
Empathy in the Face of Fear

1. Cultivating Empathy: The Foundation of the Compassion Connection
Overviews:
- Empathy serves as the cornerstone for building compassionate connections, allowing individuals to understand and share the feelings of others.
- Cultivating empathy involves recognizing and valuing diverse perspectives, fostering a deep sense of connection and understanding.
- In a compassionate community, individuals are attuned to the emotional experiences of others, creating a supportive and inclusive environment.
- Empathy plays a crucial role in fear management by promoting a sense of solidarity and shared humanity.
- Building a culture of empathy requires intentional efforts to develop emotional intelligence and interpersonal skills.

Explorations:
- Explore the impact of empathy on community well-being, mental health, and fear resilience.
- Examine cultural norms and practices that contribute to the development of empathetic individuals within communities.
- Understand the role of education in promoting empathy and fostering a compassionate mindset.
- Investigate case studies of communities that prioritize and successfully integrate empathy into their cultural fabric.
- Reflect on personal experiences where empathetic connections positively influenced fear dynamics.

Action Steps:
- Conduct workshops that focus on cultivating empathy and understanding within communities.
- Implement educational programs that teach the value of empathy from an early age.
- Launch campaigns that promote empathetic actions and behaviors within neighborhoods.
- Create platforms for individuals to share personal stories that evoke empathy and build connections.
- Encourage decision-making processes that consider and prioritize the well-being of all community members.

2. Community-Driven Support Systems: Strengthening Bonds in Times of Fear
Overviews:
- Community-driven support systems involve the collective efforts of individuals to provide emotional, practical, and social support during challenging times.
- These support systems enhance resilience, create a sense of belonging, and reinforce the notion that no one is facing fear alone.
- A compassionate community actively identifies and addresses the needs of its members, fostering a culture of mutual aid.
- In times of fear, these support systems serve as a safety net, reducing isolation and promoting a shared responsibility for well-being.
- Community-driven support systems contribute to the overall health and resilience of the community, creating a strong foundation for fear management.

Explorations:
- Explore the role of community support networks in promoting mental health and well-being.
- Examine traditional and contemporary practices that strengthen community bonds and provide support during fearful times.
- Understand the impact of cultural values and social norms on the formation and effectiveness of community-driven support systems.
- Investigate case studies of communities that have successfully implemented and sustained robust support networks.

- Reflect on personal experiences within communities where mutual aid and support were evident during challenging times.

Action Steps:

- Conduct assessments to identify the unique needs and
- Establish platforms that facilitate the exchange of support and resources among community members.
- Form teams dedicated to providing emotional support, assistance, and resources during times of fear.
- Encourage skill-sharing within communities, allowing individuals to contribute their expertise to support others.
- Implement regular check-ins and communication channels to ensure ongoing connection and support.

3. Cultivating a Culture of Forgiveness: Transforming Fear through Understanding

Overviews:

- Forgiveness is a powerful tool for transforming fear and resentment, promoting healing and reconciliation within communities.
- Cultivating a culture of forgiveness involves acknowledging the impact of fear-induced actions and seeking understanding.
- Forgiveness does not condone harmful behaviors but rather frees individuals and communities from the shackles of prolonged fear.
- A forgiving community promotes empathy, reconciliation, and collective growth, breaking the cycle of fear and retaliation.
- Forgiveness requires emotional intelligence, communication, and a commitment to building bridges across divides.

Explorations:

- Explore the psychological and societal benefits of forgiveness in reducing fear and promoting well-being.
- Examine cultural and religious perspectives on forgiveness and their impact on community dynamics.
- Understand the role of forgiveness in resolving conflicts, addressing collective traumas, and fostering peace.
- Investigate case studies of communities that have successfully embraced forgiveness as a transformative tool.
- Reflect on personal experiences where forgiveness played a role in alleviating fear and promoting understanding.

Action Steps:

- Facilitate workshops that explore the concept of forgiveness and its potential for community healing.
- Support and advocate for restorative justice initiatives that prioritize understanding and reconciliation.
- Create safe spaces for community members to engage in open dialogues, promoting understanding and forgiveness.
- Launch campaigns that highlight the transformative power of forgiveness and its impact on fear reduction.
- Develop community rituals or ceremonies that symbolize forgiveness, healing, and unity.

4. Interconnectedness with Nature: Nature-Based Approaches to Fear Management

Overviews:

- Interconnectedness with nature offers a holistic approach to fear management, connecting individuals to the natural world and its rhythms.
- Nature-based practices, such as ecotherapy and outdoor activities, have been shown to reduce stress, anxiety, and fear.
- Cultivating a sense of stewardship for the environment fosters a deeper connection with nature, promoting a fearless mindset.
- The healing power of nature provides individuals and communities with a grounding and calming influence during fearful times.
- Incorporating nature-based approaches into daily life contributes to overall well-being and resilience in the face of fear.

Explorations:

- Explore the psychological and physiological benefits of nature-based activities in reducing fear and anxiety.

- Examine cultural traditions that emphasize the connection between humans and nature for mental well-being.
- Understand the impact of urban planning and community design on the accessibility of nature and its influence on fear.
- Investigate case studies of communities that prioritize and integrate nature-based practices for fear management.
- Reflect on personal experiences of finding solace, peace, or fear reduction through interactions with the natural environment.

Action Steps:
- Advocate for the creation of green spaces and nature-inspired environments within communities.
- Support and participate in ecotherapy programs that encourage outdoor activities for mental well-being.
- Establish community gardens that provide a space for connection with nature and shared activities.
- Integrate nature-based education into school curricula and community programs.

5. Mindfulness Practices for Fear Resilience: Nurturing Present-Moment Awareness
Overviews:
- Mindfulness practices involve cultivating present-moment awareness, allowing individuals to observe thoughts and emotions without judgment.
- Mindfulness promotes resilience by reducing the grip of fear-induced thoughts and fostering a sense of clarity and calmness.
- Incorporating mindfulness into daily life enhances emotional regulation, decision-making, and overall well-being.
- A mindful community encourages the integration of mindfulness practices, creating a collective reservoir of resilience.

Explorations:
- Explore the diverse range of mindfulness practices from different cultural and spiritual traditions.
- Examine the scientific evidence supporting the benefits of mindfulness in reducing fear and anxiety.
- Understand the role of mindfulness in conflict resolution, emotional regulation, and improved decision-making.
- Investigate case studies of communities that have successfully integrated mindfulness practices into their daily lives.
- Reflect on personal experiences of the impact of mindfulness on fear resilience and well-being.

Action Steps:
- Facilitate training programs that introduce mindfulness practices to individuals and communities.
- Advocate for the integration of mindfulness programs in educational settings.
- Organize regular mindfulness sessions within the community to collectively practice and support each other.
- Support and participate in MBSR courses that teach mindfulness techniques for fear resilience.
- Conduct workshops that emphasize mindful communication, promoting understanding and reducing fear-based reactions.

Chapter 41

A Fearless Future:
Envisioning Your Life Unbound

1. Embracing Personal Growth:
Overviews:
- Personal growth involves a continuous journey of self-discovery, learning, and evolving beyond self-imposed limitations.
- It requires acknowledging strengths and weaknesses, embracing vulnerability, and fostering a mindset that welcomes change.
- Individuals committed to personal growth view challenges as opportunities for development, fueling their journey toward a fearless future.
- The process involves cultivating self-awareness, setting meaningful goals, and aligning actions with a vision for an unbound life.
- It's about becoming the best version of oneself, contributing positively to personal well-being and the surrounding community.

Explorations:
- Explore various personal development frameworks and identify those resonating with your values and aspirations.
- Reflect on the transformative experiences of individuals who embraced personal growth and overcame fears.
- Understand the role of mentors and role models in guiding one's personal growth journey.
- Examine the impact of self-reflection and mindfulness practices on fostering personal development.
- Share personal growth stories within a community to inspire and learn from collective experiences.

Action Steps:
- Craft a detailed plan outlining specific areas for growth and corresponding actions.
- Seek out mentors or role models who have navigated their own personal growth journeys.
- Establish a regular journaling habit to track progress, setbacks, and insights gained.
- Engage in activities that enhance skills and competencies aligned with personal aspirations.
- Organize or participate in workshops that facilitate collective personal growth discussions and strategies.

2. Nurturing Resilient Relationships:
Overviews:
- Resilient relationships form a cornerstone of a fearless future, providing support, understanding, and a sense of belonging.
- Building resilience within relationships involves effective communication, empathy, and shared growth.
- Individuals with resilient relationships navigate challenges together, fostering a sense of security and trust.
- These relationships contribute to emotional well-being and serve as a buffer against the uncertainties of the future.
- A fearless future is characterized by the strength of connections with friends, family, and the broader community.

Explorations:
- Explore the dynamics of resilient relationships, understanding how they withstand adversity and evolve.
- Reflect on personal experiences of overcoming relationship challenges and the lessons learned.
- Examine cultural and societal influences on relationship dynamics and resilience.
- Investigate the role of mutual goals and shared values in fostering resilient connections.
- Analyze the impact of supportive relationships on individual and collective fear reduction.

Action Steps:

- Engage in workshops focusing on effective communication and conflict resolution.
- Plan retreats or activities that strengthen bonds and create shared memories.
- Cultivate a habit of expressing gratitude within relationships to reinforce positive connections.
- Regularly assess and discuss the state of relationships, addressing concerns openly.
- Establish or contribute to community support networks that encourage resilient relationships.

3. Mastering Personal Finance:

Overviews:
- Financial stability is a key pillar of a fearless future, providing a sense of security and empowerment.
- Understanding financial principles, budgeting, and investing are crucial for long-term financial well-being.
- Individuals with financial literacy are better equipped to face unexpected challenges and pursue opportunities.
- A fearless future involves making informed financial decisions that align with personal and collective goals.
- Financial mastery contributes to reduced anxiety about the future and fosters a mindset of abundance.

Explorations:
- Explore the impact of financial stress on mental health and overall well-being.
- Examine successful financial management strategies adopted by individuals who have overcome adversity.
- Investigate cultural and societal attitudes toward money and their influence on financial habits.
- Reflect on personal experiences of financial challenges and the lessons learned.
- Analyze the connection between financial education, empowerment, and fear reduction.

Action Steps:
- Enroll in courses or workshops to enhance financial literacy and understanding.
- Implement effective budgeting practices to manage income, expenses, and savings.
- Learn about investment opportunities and strategies for long-term financial growth.
- Establish and contribute to an emergency fund for unforeseen circumstances.
- Engage with financial planners to create personalized financial plans aligned with fearless living.

4. Nurturing Physical Well-being:

Overviews:
- Physical health is a foundational element for realizing a fearless future, influencing overall quality of life.
- Prioritizing exercise, nutrition, and adequate rest contributes to resilience in facing life's challenges.
- Individuals who prioritize their physical well-being are more likely to cope effectively with stress and fear.
- A fearless future involves cultivating habits that promote long-term physical health and vitality.
- Physical well-being is interconnected with mental and emotional wellness, forming a holistic approach to fear reduction.

Explorations:
- Explore the impact of regular exercise on mental clarity, emotional stability, and stress reduction.
- Examine the role of nutrition in providing energy, supporting immune function, and enhancing mood.
- Investigate mindfulness practices and their positive effects on physical and mental well-being.
- Reflect on personal experiences where physical health has played a role in fear management.
- Analyze cultural perspectives on physical well-being and their influence on lifestyle choices.

Action Steps:
- Establish a regular exercise routine that aligns with personal preferences and goals.
- Learn about balanced nutrition and make informed choices for a healthy diet.
- Incorporate mindfulness activities such as meditation or yoga into daily life.
- Schedule regular check-ups to monitor and maintain physical health.
- Develop healthy sleep habits to ensure adequate and restful sleep for optimal well-being.

5. Cultivating Emotional Resilience:

Overviews:
- Emotional resilience is a key element in navigating challenges and uncertainties with courage.
- Understanding and managing emotions contribute to a more stable and fearless mindset.

- Resilient individuals are better equipped to bounce back from setbacks and adapt to change.
- Cultivating emotional intelligence involves recognizing, understanding, and harnessing emotions constructively.
- A fearless future embraces emotional resilience as a vital component of personal growth and well-being.

Explorations:
- Explore the role of self-awareness in understanding emotional triggers and responses.
- Examine the impact of positive thinking and optimism on emotional resilience.
- Investigate effective strategies for managing stress and preventing emotional burnout.
- Reflect on personal experiences where emotional resilience played a crucial role in overcoming fear.
- Analyze the cultural influences on emotional expression and coping mechanisms.

Action Steps:
- Engage in regular journaling to enhance self-awareness and emotional expression.
- Incorporate positive affirmations to foster an optimistic mindset.
- Learn and practice stress management techniques such as deep breathing or meditation.
- Seek therapeutic support or counseling for developing emotional resilience.
- Participate in cultural sensitivity training to understand diverse emotional expressions.

Chapter 42

Becoming a Fearless Mentor:
Sharing Your Journey with Others

1. Becoming a Fearless Mentor: Sharing Your Journey with Others
Overviews:
- Embracing the role of a mentor involves sharing personal experiences and insights, creating a meaningful connection with mentees.
- Fearless mentoring is rooted in authenticity, transparency, and vulnerability, fostering a safe space for mentees to explore their own fears and aspirations.
- A fearless mentor serves as a guide, providing encouragement, constructive feedback, and a roadmap for navigating challenges.
- Mentoring is a reciprocal journey; both mentor and mentee contribute to each other's growth, creating a symbiotic relationship.
- Fearless mentors inspire courage, resilience, and a sense of possibility, empowering mentees to overcome obstacles and pursue their aspirations.

Explorations:
- Explore your own journey, identifying pivotal moments of fear, challenges overcome, and lessons learned to share with mentees.
- Examine successful mentorship stories, understanding the dynamics of effective communication, trust-building, and mutual respect.
- Understand the unique fears and aspirations of potential mentees, tailoring your mentoring approach to individual needs.
- Reflect on the qualities of mentors who have positively impacted your life, extracting valuable insights for your own mentoring style.
- Explore diverse mentoring models and techniques, incorporating adaptable strategies to suit different mentee personalities and goals.

Action Steps:
- Establish structured mentorship programs within your community or workplace.
- Conduct workshops on effective mentoring, emphasizing the importance of fearless communication.
- Create resources such as guides, toolkits, or online platforms to support mentors and mentees.
- Foster a culture of peer mentoring, promoting collaboration and shared learning among peers.
- Arrange events that facilitate networking and mentoring connections, expanding opportunities for mentorship.

2. Building Resilience through Mindful Practices: Nurturing Inner Strength
Overviews:
- Building resilience involves cultivating a mindset that views challenges as opportunities for growth and learning.
- Mindful practices, such as meditation and self-reflection, enhance self-awareness and provide a foundation for emotional resilience.
- Resilience is a dynamic process; it involves adapting positively to adversity and bouncing back from setbacks with newfound strength.
- Mindfulness contributes to a balanced and focused mindset, enabling individuals to navigate fear and uncertainty more effectively.

Explorations:
- Explore various mindfulness techniques, including meditation, deep breathing, and mindfulness-based stress reduction.
- Examine case studies of individuals who have built resilience through mindfulness, understanding the transformative impact on their lives.
- Understand the intersection of mindfulness and emotional intelligence, recognizing emotions without being overwhelmed by them.

- Explore the connection between physical well-being, mental health, and resilience, recognizing the holistic nature of resilience-building.

Action Steps:
- Incorporate short mindfulness practices into daily activities to develop a consistent routine.
- Organize workshops to introduce mindfulness techniques and provide guidance on integrating them into daily life.
- Develop resources such as guided meditation recordings or informational materials to support mindfulness practices.
- Encourage the formation of communities or groups focused on mindfulness, fostering shared learning and support.

3. Embracing Change as a Catalyst for Growth: A Fearless Approach to Transformation

Overviews:
- Embracing change involves adopting a mindset that views it as a natural and inevitable part of life's journey.
- Fearless individuals approach change with curiosity and optimism, recognizing it as an opportunity for personal and collective growth.
- The ability to adapt to change is a key component of resilience, allowing individuals to thrive in dynamic and uncertain environments.
- Fear of change often stems from a fear of the unknown; reframing perspectives can turn change into a source of excitement and possibility.
- Cultivating a fearless approach to change involves developing a mindset that values flexibility, adaptability, and continuous learning.

Explorations:
- Explore psychological theories on the fear of change, understanding the cognitive and emotional factors that influence perceptions.
- Examine case studies of individuals or communities that have navigated significant changes successfully, identifying key strategies.
- Understand the role of organizational culture in fostering adaptability and innovation in the face of change.
- Explore the concept of a growth mindset and its relationship to embracing change as an opportunity for personal and professional development.

Action Steps:
- Conduct workshops focused on building change-readiness skills, including adaptability and open-mindedness.
- Establish mentorship programs where experienced individuals guide others through navigating and embracing change.
- Develop resources that provide practical tips and insights on effectively managing and embracing change.
- Encourage a culture where individuals and organizations learn from past changes to improve future responses.
- Advocate for the inclusion of modules on change resilience in educational curricula.

4. Fearless Communication: Building Authentic Connections in a Digital World

Overviews:
- Fearless communication involves expressing thoughts, feelings, and ideas authentically and transparently.
- In a digital world, effective communication is crucial for building genuine connections and fostering understanding.
- Fear of judgment or rejection often hinders authentic communication; overcoming this fear is essential for meaningful interactions.
- Fearless communicators actively listen, empathize, and convey their messages with clarity and intention.
- Building strong communication skills enhances relationships, both personally and professionally.

Explorations:
- Explore the impact of digital communication on interpersonal relationships and identify challenges and opportunities.

- Examine case studies of individuals or organizations that have successfully navigated digital communication challenges, emphasizing authenticity.
- Understand the psychological barriers that hinder authentic communication, such as the fear of vulnerability or misinterpretation.
- Explore different communication styles and identify the factors that contribute to effective and impactful communication.

Action Steps:
- Conduct workshops focused on developing effective and authentic communication skills.
- Provide training on empathetic communication in digital spaces, emphasizing the nuances of online interaction.
- Create environments, both online and offline, where individuals feel safe expressing themselves authentically.
- Promote a culture that values vulnerability as a strength, fostering deeper and more meaningful connections.
- Develop guidelines and best practices for digital communication to enhance clarity and understanding.

5. Fearless Growth: Embracing Change and Continuous Evolution

Overviews:
- Fearless growth involves a mindset that welcomes change, challenges, and opportunities for continuous evolution.
- Embracing change requires resilience, adaptability, and a willingness to step outside of one's comfort zone.
- Fearless individuals view setbacks as opportunities to learn, grow, and refine their path toward personal and collective success.
- Continuous evolution involves an ongoing commitment to self-improvement, skill development, and the pursuit of new experiences.
- A fearless approach to growth enables individuals to thrive in dynamic environments and navigate uncertainties with confidence.

Explorations:
- Explore the psychological and emotional aspects of embracing change and its impact on personal well-being.
- Examine case studies of individuals or organizations that have effectively embraced change and leveraged it for positive growth.
- Understand the role of a growth mindset in fostering resilience and adaptability in the face of challenges.
- Investigate the connection between continuous learning, innovation, and fearless growth in various life domains.

Action Steps:
- Organize seminars that explore the benefits of embracing change and continuous evolution.
- Encourage individuals to create personalized plans for continuous self-improvement and growth.
- Support initiatives that facilitate the acquisition of new skills and knowledge for personal and professional development.
- Develop programs that focus on building resilience as a core skill for fearless growth.

Chapter 43

Beyond the Shadow of Fear:
Steps into the Sunshine of Fearless Living

1. Embracing Fear as a Catalyst for Growth
Overviews:
- Acknowledge fear as a natural emotion that can serve as a powerful catalyst for personal and transformative growth.
- Embrace the mindset that viewing fear as a teacher rather than an obstacle can lead to valuable insights and self-discovery.
- Recognize that stepping into the unknown, guided by fear, can foster resilience, adaptability, and a deeper understanding of oneself.
- Understand that the journey beyond fear involves self-compassion and the acceptance of vulnerability.
- Cultivate a fearless attitude by reframing fear as an opportunity for courage, strength, and positive change.

Explorations:
- Explore personal stories or anecdotes where individuals have turned moments of fear into transformative experiences.
- Examine psychological theories or studies that highlight the positive effects of embracing fear for personal development.
- Engage in reflective practices to understand the specific fears that may be hindering personal growth.
- Investigate philosophical perspectives on fear and courage, drawing inspiration from various cultural or historical sources.
- Explore different mindfulness and meditation techniques to develop a deeper awareness of one's fears.

Action Steps:
- Document fears, reflecting on their origins and potential lessons for personal growth.
- Share fears and growth experiences with a trusted friend or mentor for mutual support.
- Participate in workshops or seminars focused on understanding and overcoming fears.
- Identify specific fears and set gradual, achievable goals to confront and overcome them.
- Gradually expose yourself to manageable levels of feared situations, building resilience over time.

2. Building Resilience through Fearful Challenges
Overviews:
- Acknowledge that challenges born from fear can be transformative opportunities to build resilience.
- Understand that overcoming smaller fears can contribute to the development of a resilient mindset for larger challenges.
- View resilience as the ability to adapt positively to adversity and fear, fostering mental and emotional strength.
- Recognize that building resilience involves learning from failures and setbacks on the path to fearless living.
- Cultivate a mindset that perceives challenges as invitations to grow rather than insurmountable obstacles.

Explorations:
- Explore case studies or biographies of individuals who have demonstrated resilience in the face of fear.
- Examine the psychological components of resilience and its impact on mental well-being.
- Reflect on personal experiences of overcoming challenges and the resulting growth.
- Investigate various therapeutic approaches that focus on building resilience and coping with fear.
- Engage in conversations with resilient individuals to understand their strategies and perspectives.

Action Steps:
- Incorporate daily exercises that promote mental and emotional resilience.
- Compile resources, activities, and strategies that help navigate and overcome challenges.
- Set intentional challenges that gradually expose you to feared situations, fostering resilience.

- Connect with mentors who have demonstrated resilience, seeking guidance in navigating challenges.
- Acknowledge and celebrate achievements, no matter how small, to reinforce a resilient mindset.

3. Rewriting Fearful Narratives: The Power of Self-Storytelling
Overviews:
- Recognize the influence of personal narratives in shaping the perception of fear.
- Understand that narratives can either amplify or diminish the impact of fear on one's life.
- Acknowledge the power of self-storytelling in redefining the relationship with fear.
- Cultivate a conscious narrative that emphasizes personal strengths, resilience, and the capacity for growth.
- Use storytelling as a tool for self-empowerment and a means to inspire others on their fearless journey.

Explorations:
- Explore literature or literature therapy that focuses on transforming fear through narrative.
- Examine the role of cultural or societal narratives in shaping individual attitudes toward fear.
- Reflect on personal narratives, identifying recurring themes and patterns related to fear.
- Investigate the impact of positive affirmations and self-talk in altering fearful narratives.
- Engage in narrative therapy techniques or workshops to actively rewrite fear-related stories.

Action Steps:
- Address fears in writing, reframing them as opportunities for growth and learning.
- Develop and recite daily affirmations that challenge negative fear-based narratives.
- Openly share personal stories of overcoming fear to inspire and connect with others.
- Join workshops or groups focused on reshaping personal narratives.

4. Cultivating Fearless Connections: Nurturing Supportive Relationships
Overviews:
- Recognize the impact of social connections on fear management and personal growth.
- Understand that supportive relationships can provide emotional safety and encouragement to face fears.
- Acknowledge the importance of vulnerability in cultivating deep, meaningful connections.
- Cultivate a network of individuals who share a commitment to fearless living.
- Embrace the idea that fear can be collectively navigated, strengthening bonds and fostering a sense of community.

Explorations:
- Explore research on the role of social support in managing stress and fear.
- Reflect on past relationships to identify patterns of support or hindrance in fear management.
- Investigate the concept of vulnerability as a cornerstone of authentic connections.
- Examine different models of supportive communities that promote fearless living.
- Engage in conversations with individuals who have successfully navigated fear within a supportive network.

Action Steps:
- Assess the quality and diversity of your social connections, identifying areas for expansion or strengthening.
- Explore joining clubs, groups, or online communities that align with your interests to foster new connections.
- Practice expressing vulnerability within your trusted social circles, gradually sharing fears and concerns.
- Be mindful of the impact of social interactions on your mood and fear levels, adjusting as needed.
- Establish healthy boundaries in social interactions, ensuring a balance between connection and personal space.

5. Fearless Mindfulness: Cultivating Present-Moment Awareness
Overviews:
- Acknowledge the role of mindfulness in managing fear by fostering present-moment awareness.
- Understand that fear often arises from anticipation of future events or past traumas, which mindfulness can mitigate.
- Cultivate the ability to observe and accept fear without judgment, creating space for conscious responses.

- Recognize that a fearless life is built upon a foundation of intentional, mindful living.
- Embrace mindfulness as a tool for grounding oneself during moments of fear, promoting clarity and resilience.

Explorations:
- Explore mindfulness practices such as meditation, breathwork, or mindful walking to understand their impact on fear.
- Examine scientific studies on the neurological and psychological effects of mindfulness on fear.
- Reflect on personal experiences where mindfulness has positively influenced fear responses.
- Investigate mindfulness traditions from different cultures and their perspectives on fear.
- Engage in mindfulness retreats or workshops to deepen your practice.

Action Steps:
- Dedicate time each day to mindfulness practices that resonate with you.
- Incorporate conscious breathing during moments of fear to center yourself.
- Practice observing fear without immediate reaction, allowing space for understanding.
- Connect with a friend or partner to mutually support and encourage mindful living.
- Explore local or online programs that offer guidance and structure for cultivating mindfulness in daily life.

www.ingramcontent.com/pod-product-compliance
Lightning Source LLC
Chambersburg PA
CBHW080850120626

46546CB00008B/2766